TRINITY
OF MAN

TRINITY OF MAN

by

Dennis and Rita Bennett

Logos International
Plainfield, New Jersey

Quotes from the Authorized Version of the Bible have in most places been modernized by the authors in keeping with the original meanings.

The characters portrayed in the first seven chapters of this book are fictitious, and any resemblance to any person, living or dead, is purely coincidental. Names and incidental circumstances in other illustrations have sometimes been changed.

This book is lovingly dedicated to the memory of

WILLIAM HARVEY REED.

He was faithful unto death and

received a crown of life.

Acknowledgments

Loving thanks to God for the ministry of the late Pastor C.A. Brown, who shared what it means to be new creatures in Christ, and for the late Watchman Nee, whose books have pioneered in the field of the triune person.

Thanks to our families and friends who have prayed so often for us as we have been writing this book.

Special thanks to our friend and secretary, Janet Koether, who labored with us long and hard right up to the last lines of this manuscript. Thanks also to a new friend, Cynthia Anderson, who typed for us while we were in Tampa, Florida.

Thanks and praise most of all to our Lord Jesus Christ. Without Him this book couldn't have been conceived or written. Without Him there would be no life in the Spirit, and no healing or changing of the soul which this book tells about.

Preface

Following a speaking engagement, a little man came up to me and said happily, "I really enjoyed reading that book you wrote. You know, the one that has your wife's name on it, too!" He was referring to *The Holy Spirit and You* which Rita and I co-authored in 1971.

I realized he wasn't trying to be offensive, so I just replied firmly, "My friend, when my wife and I put our names on a book it means we have written it *together!*"

Rita and I enjoy a real partnership in the Lord. When we married in 1966 (I had been a widower for three years, and Rita had never married), we each had our own ministry, and the Lord brought our ministries together. Since then most of the time we work as a team.

We enjoy reading about another husband and wife team in the New Testament, Aquila and Priscilla. They were close friends of the Apostle Paul. It's interesting to note that Paul sometimes addresses them as "Aquila and Priscilla" and sometimes as "Priscilla and Aquila." Luke, too, in the Acts of the Apostles, uses the names in either order. Apparently, contrary to popular belief, Paul wasn't defensive about male superiority, and neither was Luke!

The inspiration for this book, and most of its basic material, came from Rita. It was she who first interested me in the importance of recognizing the "trinity of man." She had been studying the subject long before we were married.

We've been teaching on the topic for some twelve years now, and the Lord has given both of us further insights and illustrations which we have tried to share here.

As we work, I write a chapter and Rita revises and edits it. Rita writes a chapter, and I revise and edit it. We may pass a chapter back and forth many times before we are satisfied with it. It isn't always easy. You've got to love one another a lot to work this way, but that's the way our co-authored books are written, and I'd like you to know as you read them that they are truly a product of the shared ministry the Lord has given Dennis and Rita Bennett. Praise Him!

Dennis J. Bennett
Edmonds, Washington
August 25, 1979

Contents

TRINITY
OF MAN

1

Monday Morning Blues

"... Early morning fog in the coastal areas. Good Morning! This is radio station, KJCO, 1300 kilohertz and the time is 6:45."

Bill Carter groped for the button to shut off the artificial cheerfulness of the announcer. The alarm-radio subsided and Bill lay dozing awhile, then gathering willpower, he threw back the bedclothes and sat blinking at the sunbeams that patterned the carpet. Monday morning! He glanced at the clock again—7:00! Heavens! And he had to catch the 7:40!

"What time is it?" Carol likewise emerged from the covers where she had been curled, trying to ignore the new day.

"Late," said her husband, briefly. "You'd better hop out of the sack and get us a bite to eat. Don't have much time."

"Why didn't you set the alarm earlier?" Carol's voice was a little grumpy.

"Because we stayed out too late last night, that's why!"

"We had a good time, though," said his wife, throwing on her robe, and pushing back her curly brown hair.

A wail from elsewhere demanded immediate attention. "Mom! Billy's taken my hairbrush again! Make him give it back!" Carol sighed as she left the bedroom to unsquabble Jane and Billy, the two youngest Carters.

"Yeah, it was a good time last night," said Bill, as Carol returned, having brought uneasy peace to the children's bathroom. "But how come I can go to bed feeling great and wake up feeling crummy? And you don't look the exact picture of joy yourself, you know that?"

"Uh-huh," Carol assented. "Well, I'm not going to let it bother me, anyway."

It did bother her, though, as she thought it over after Bill had swept hastily through toast and coffee, and departed for the office, and the two young Carters had been edged off to school, still complaining. It *had* been a good time last night, and this morning it wasn't.

Buttering another piece of toast, Carol pondered further. Typical of many young Americans, she, like Bill, had been duly baptized shortly after her arrival into the world. She was sent with fair regularity to Sunday school as soon as she was old enough. Her agnostic parents thought it might "do her some good." Perhaps it had, Carol thought, taking a sip of coffee. She had graduated from Sunday school to the youth group, and it was there she had met Bill. They had been married at that same church and had continued to attend occasionally. Bill wasn't very interested though and said so. "I can read most of the stuff in the paper that I hear from that pulpit," he said. "Seems to me we had more religion in the youth group—at least they talked about God and Jesus now and then!"

Carol was more sympathetic. "I hear what Pastor

Wilkes is saying," she said. "And he's right as far as it goes. We ought to be more concerned about minorities and their problems, and about the things the big industries are up to, and about war, and all that sort of thing, but somehow it's mostly talk. Nobody seems to *do* anything much."

Bill had chuckled at that. "Pastor Wilkes took part in that protest march last year—what was it about? 'Don't buy grapes,' or 'Stop the ITT' or something like that. Got himself in hot water with some of the congregation, didn't he?"

Carol nodded. "Uh-huh, but that's what I mean. It took a lot of guts for him to do that. It's obvious that not many people sitting listening to him were with him. It's a sort of solo act."

"There aren't very many listening to him, anyway. That church is dying on the vine, Carol. There were less than fifty there the last time we went."

So it had created a bit of sensation when Carol asked one night after supper if Bill would like to attend a neighborhood prayer meeting with her. She could still see the look of surprise on his face as he put down his coffee cup.

"Now hold it, honey," he said. *"Prayer* meeting? No thank you! I went to one once years ago, when I was visiting grandma. I was too small to defend myself! It was in her little old church in the country, and it was *dull!* All I remember is people getting up and telling their troubles to the Lord, but they didn't sound as though they expected He would do anything about them. Boy, those were long prayers, and I remember how sad everyone looked. Well, there was one old boy who told about how he'd had some kind of experience with God years before—his face had

3

brightened up while he talked about it. That impressed me. I'm just not the prayer meeting type, Carol, and anyway, what's a prayer meeting doing at *that* church?"

"But Bill, this isn't at a church. It's at Bob and Sue Jensen's. You know, the big house down the street!"

Bill's expression had changed. "Jensen's?" he said incredulously. "But he's the vice president of Jensen and Stirling, the architects! One of our best accounts. He's quite a guy. You don't mean to tell me he's letting his wife have *prayer meetings* at their house?"

"No, dear, not his wife; or not *just* her. It's *him* and her. Bob runs the meeting, I'm told. When I saw Sue at PTA recently, she invited us."

Bill had thoughtfully poured himself another cup of coffee. "H'm. Well, I guess it couldn't do any harm. It might even be good for business and my boss wouldn't mind that at all! Oh, I wouldn't go for that reason," Bill added quickly, as Carol's face clouded, "I was just kidding. If you want to go, I'll go with you. But let's sit near the door, just in case things get too sticky. Okay?"

2

Lost and Found

They found themselves in a crowded front room at the Jensen home. Carol looked around for some sign of church authority, and spotted a black shirt and white collar on a young-looking man sitting in a corner. She remembered that the Jensens were Episcopalians and this was probably their priest. When the proceedings began though, it wasn't the man with the clerical collar who took the lead, but Bob Jensen. They sang some songs, and it was fun! More like popular music than the hymns she remembered from church. And the people sure did sing! Carol stole a peek at her husband, and to her amazement *he* was making an effort to join in!

After they had sung awhile, something a bit more scary happened. Bob said, "Let's praise God!" and they had proceeded to do it! Good heavens! Carol remembered enough of her brief church career to know what *praise* was. It meant singing a hymn slowly and sadly, reading a Psalm, "going to church" in general. But these people seemed to have a somewhat different concept. They all

joined in, and as a chorus of voices rose around her—
"Thank you, God! Jesus, you're wonderful! Praise
God!"—she felt a little like beating a retreat. She glanced
at Bill. Surely he'd never survive *this;* but he had his head
down and his eyes closed. Then she noticed that several
people actually had their hands lifted as she'd seen in
some old Bible pictures. The woman next to her did, and
Carol knew her. She was the wife of a professional man in
town, herself a leader in local "society." Perhaps the thing
that kept Carol from complete panic was the radiant look
on this woman's face!

"There are some of you here," Bob said, when the voices
of praise had diminished, "who don't have much use for
religion and church. Okay. Let's not talk about that. Sue
and I go to church—we're Episcopalians," he grinned at
the young priest. "Father Waters knows that. But the
heart of the matter, the nitty-gritty, isn't whether you go to
church or have some kind of religious belief, but whether
you've gotten to know God as your friend.

"Some of you are pretty lonesome and scared in this old
world. You don't know who you are, or where you're
going or what it's all about. That's called being 'lost.' You
know you need forgiving, too, for the ornery things you've
said and done. Some of you are having a go at
Transcendental Meditation, or something like that to see
if you can get some peace and joy. Some of you think
you're going to buy happiness, if you can just get enough
money for a new house, or a new car, or a boat, or
something, but those of you who have already 'made it' in
business know that isn't the answer either. Take me, for
instance. I'm not rich, but I've got enough. I've got a great
family, a nice home, and all kinds of things, but up until a
couple of years ago I was miserable. I invited some of you

to join us tonight because I wanted to share what happened to me."

Bill was listening very closely.

"I always thought Christianity was a matter of keeping rules," Bob went on. "You know, being honest in business, good to your neighbors, and all that. Jesus Christ to me was someone up in 'heaven,' or a figure in the Bible. I guess I always imagined Him in a long white robe with a long sad face, long hair, long beard—I'm sure a lot of you know what I'm talking about.

"Religion was, well, kind of old-fashioned and stuffy, and probably on the way out. But it was still part of being 100 percent American—believing in God, and mother, and all that—and I wasn't enough of a rebel to make waves. I went along to church with my wife, Sue, quite often, gave a little money, even served on the vestry for a term. I thought, 'Well, if there is anything to this business of God and religion, at least I'm keeping my foot in the door, and paying my dues!' " Bob paused and thought a moment. "But I was still unhappy inside. Life seemed to have less and less meaning as the days went by. You know what was the matter with me? I was lonesome. Oh, sure, I had a nice wife and family, and lots of good friends, well, acquaintances anyway, but inside I was lonesome for something, and I didn't know what.

"Then while I was on a business trip upstate I met a businessman who talked about Jesus Christ like He was right-here-and-now real. I asked him, 'How did you get that way?' He said, 'I just asked Jesus to make Himself real to me, and He did! Why don't you try it and see for yourself?'

"Somehow I believed the man. I knew I needed what he obviously had, so although I felt pretty silly, I said, 'Jesus, if you're real, and can do something for me, please let me know.' And He *did!* I found He's real and alive, and all of a sudden my life has purpose and meaning. I know who I am, and where I'm going, and what it's all about. It wasn't religion I needed, but a relationship. I asked Him to forgive me for the bad things I'd done, and now I can ask Him to forgive me whenever I go wrong—which is quite often! I don't have to carry a load of guilt around with me.

"Now, of course, the church I belonged to had talked about forgiveness and so forth, but somehow no one had ever asked me to close the deal with the Lord."

Bob paused for quite a few moments, then he said, "Look, I have a hunch there are some of you here who are feeling like I was, and I want to challenge you to try an experiment. Let's make it real simple. You all close your eyes so no one will feel embarrassed, and then anyone who would like to, may say, 'Jesus, if you are real, please let me know. Forgive me for all the wrong things I've done, and come into my life. I'd like to accept you, Jesus.' Simply stick up your hand, like you were voting 'yes' in a committee meeting! See what happens."

Carol ducked her head and closed her eyes. Something inside her was saying: "It's true, what he's talking about. You need to know it too." Hesitantly, she raised her hand. As she did, the strangest, most wonderful sense of well-being flooded through her. It was a feeling that combined warmth and joy and peace, just like somehow she knew everything was going to be okay. Under her breath she said, "Jesus, you truly are real! Thank you! I do accept you." Right away the thought came: "Bill mustn't miss this. He needs it too." She was going to whisper to him, to try to tell him what had just happened to her, when she realized to her delighted surprise that he had his hand raised too!

8

3

Something More— And the Result

That was how it had begun. Going home from the Jensens' that night they had both realized they were different. And the next day it was the same. They started going regularly to their church, although it was difficult. "I just feel God wants us there," Carol commented, and Bill agreed. They shared their experience with their minister, and he showed some interest. "You've had a conversion," he commented. "That's good! Some people do. I'm glad for you," he said, a little wistfully.

After a few months, it was Bill who first said, "You know, honey, that was real—accepting Jesus. Something truly happened, but I'm sort of losing track of it. I asked the pastor what was the matter with me, and he said, 'Oh, you're just cooling off! You don't expect to be on a spiritual high all the time, do you?' To which my answer would have been, 'Well, yes, as a matter of fact, I do! I need to be, in the kind of world I live in!' And Carol, you know those Jensens, and the other people who meet with them, they have something else, something more—I know they do."

Carol had agreed, because it was obvious. "I've been feeling for some time we ought to have gone back to the Jensens," she commented. "They had more to tell us, but I didn't say anything."

So they had cornered Bob and Sue. "Well, yes," Bob said, "we sure do have more to tell you. I was going to drop by your office, and suggest that you come back over to our house some evening, but somehow I never got around to it. I'm sorry. You got the first half of the deal, now you need the rest! Look, why don't you come over tonight, and we'll talk about it. Okay?"

That night Bob and Sue explained to them about the baptism in the Holy Spirit, the experience of Pentecost. They shared how the new life they had been given when they received Jesus had been released to fill them with even greater love and joy. This had made them much more aware of God, and able to let Him work through them, sometimes in miraculous ways.

They had done more than talk about it; Carol and Bill had asked Jesus to baptize them in the Holy Spirit and He had done so. They both spoke in new languages, just as the apostles did, and joy and reality had flooded them in a way they could not have imagined possible. Carol wept buckets of happy tears, while Bill laughed and cried all at the same time. He was so overwhelmed with the joy of the Lord that for a little while he could hardly stand up!

"You'd better be careful on your way home," Bob kidded. "You don't want to be arrested for drunken driving!"

It had been an incredible evening, and the days that followed were incredible too. Both of them would awaken in the morning full of praise for God and love for one another and the children (who were a little baffled by it all at first). Even in the middle of the day, God was still so amazingly real to them. Bill found he could talk about Jesus to people when opportunities came during the business day. He found he could even love his boss—who was a bit of a Scrooge. Carol was so radiant that her back-fence neighbor asked her the very first day, "What's come over you, Carol?" Carol had told her what had happened, and led her to Jesus and the baptism in the Holy Spirit!

Religion was no longer a private matter. Before, even though they had both received Jesus, they still had been hesitant to talk about Him. Now they had freedom to talk and pray together. When they went to the meeting at the Jensens', which they now began to do every week, sometimes the sense of God's presence would be so real they felt they could reach out and touch Him.

Even the services in their church seemed different—there seemed to be more meaning to them. And the Bible! Well, it just "lit up like a Christmas tree" as Bill put it.

And it was more than feelings! When they prayed, things happened! There was an old lady down the street—Carol was casually acquainted with her. The woman was pretty badly crippled with arthritis, and had a heart condition which kept her confined to her bed much of the time, but she was a keen old lady with a twinkle in her eye. One day Carol stopped by to see how she was doing. "Oh, yes," said the woman, in response to Carol's inquiries about her health, "I've got this angina and this pesky rheumatism—it keeps me down most of the time. Don't like it, but there it is! God's will, I guess, and I sure can't do much about that!"

At this last remark Carol found herself saying: "Nonsense! God doesn't want you flat on your back! He doesn't want you sick—that's not His will for you!"

The old lady's eyes had widened. "What are you talking about, my dear? Have you taken up Christian Science or something?"

"No," Carol had replied. "Not Christian Science; just Christianity. Look, would you mind if I prayed and asked Jesus to make you well?"

Old Mrs. Cooper stared at her younger friend for quite a while, then replied slowly, "No, I guess not. Go ahead." Carol had never done anything like this before, but she took the old lady's hand in both of hers and said simply: "Jesus, I know you don't want my friend to be sick and hurting, so please heal her. Thank you." Her courage collapsed, and she left rather hastily. "I was afraid to ask her how she felt," she explained later.

The next week, while Carol was vacuuming the front room rug, there was a knock at the door. She opened it to find Mrs. Cooper standing there with a big smile on her face. "Hi, honey, I just brought you some cookies I baked," She waved the bag in her hand.

"C—come in," Carol stammered, watching with amazement the agility with which her neighbor negotiated the steps. "Why, you really look much better!"

"Better?" the old lady chortled. "Look at what I can do!" She then proceeded to execute a few dance steps across the floor, and came back and hugged Carol. "Thank you! Thank you so much for that prayer. It worked! Now tell me more about it all. How did you find out? What's been happening?" Carol told her the whole story.

"Okay," said Mrs. Cooper gaily, "I'm ready."

"Y—you're ready for what?"

"To receive the baptism in the Holy Spirit, of course! I

12

always knew there was something more to this Christianity business. I accepted Jesus when I was just a girl, but they didn't tell me what came next. I'm not getting any younger, and there's no time to waste. I want what you've got!" And Carol had her first experience of praying with someone for the release of the Holy Spirit. Mrs. Cooper, like the Ethiopian of old (Acts 8:39), had "gone on her way rejoicing"!

Then the kids started getting involved. Carol and Bill had been hesitant to say anything to their son Tony, who was just entering college. He hadn't been very impressed by religion up to this point; in fact, he rather prided himself on his agnosticism, but the very day after his parents had received the baptism in the Holy Spirit, Tony had questioned them at the supper table. "What's with you guys? Some new kind of tranquilizer, or somethin'? Gosh, you both act like you've got the world by the tail!" This had led to a very interesting evening, which ended by Tony accepting Jesus, and receiving the Holy Spirit.

To everyone's surprise, the twins were next. Bill and Carol had started having family prayers after Tony received Jesus and the baptism in the Holy Spirit, and one evening as the three of them were quietly praying in the Spirit, they had been not a little surprised to realize that the two eight-year-olds were happily praying along with them! It seemed as natural as breathing.

People came across their path in new ways, sometimes in startling ways! One night there was a bad wreck right in front of their house. In fact, one of the cars had ended up on their front lawn. Several people had been injured—fortunately no one had been killed. Carol and Bill spent the whole evening helping in one way or another—coffee, telephone, errands, comforting people, praying.

Praying! Carol chuckled to herself as she remembered what she used to think about that! "Let's pray, there's nothing else we can do. It sure can't do any harm, and might do some good!" Now prayer had become a real weapon, effective and powerful.

She and Bill would not soon forget the fellow trapped in the front seat of one of the cars with his leg folded under him and twisted like a pretzel. The men sprung the door open and carefully extricated him. The medic pronounced the leg badly fractured, and made the man as comfortable as possible while he went on to the next person.

Bill and Carol asked, "Do you mind if we pray for that leg?"

The man looked surprised, but grunted, "Naw. Can't hurt any more than it does already. Go ahead."

When Bill laid his hands on the leg, he actually felt it straighten out! The man suddenly sat up. "What did you do?" he exclaimed. "It quit hurting! Why, I believe I can use it!" He struggled to his feet and began to walk around, in dazed amazement—an amazement that was shared by Bill and Carol. The ambulance took the man to the hospital, but they could find no sign of any fracture. The happy sequel was that he had come back to talk with Bill and Carol, and had accepted Jesus for himself, and received the power of the Holy Spirit too.

"Last year," Bill commented, "I'd have tried every which way to ignore that mess on the front lawn. If I could, I'd have turned out all the lights, and pretended there was no one at home! I wouldn't have had the least idea what to do or say to those people, but now it's different. The words were there when I needed them, and I seemed to know what to do."

And so it went—time after time they had opportunities to help others. Most wonderful of all was the love that seemed to flow so easily now. Carol and Bill had always had a good relationship, with a minimum of battles, but now they seemed to be on a "second honeymoon." Even the twins, who normally quarreled at least twice a day, now rarely made a fuss. The new awareness of God they all felt made everything different. Certainly life had never been so exciting and adventurous.

4

Cooling Down

Carol's heart warmed as she thought back over these things. But sadness came when she pondered how the same thing had begun to happen that had happened after they received Jesus—they were cooling down. There wasn't any doubt that they were both different than they had been before receiving the power of the Holy Spirit, but they were losing out in some way. Prayers weren't being answered the way they had been at first. Sometimes it was hard to remember the exciting events of just a few months before. Life seemed to be dropping back into the old routine, illuminated now only briefly with that wonderful sense of God's presence. Sometimes at the meeting at the Jensens'—they still attended faithfully— there would be a tremendous lift of joy. They'd had a wonderful time last night, Carol reminisced, and on the way home they had been laughing and praising God together, but it sure didn't seem to last.

Old problems were coming back. Carol thought her bad dreams had gone for good, but now they had started again. Bill had thought his attitude had changed toward his boss and his job. He had also thought he could avoid flirting with one or two of the cuter secretaries, but the old feelings were back again.

One of their friends had volunteered an explanation: "You're just settling down for the long haul," he had said. "God gave you these exciting things to get your attention. It was a sort of childhood, and those were the toys. Now you're growing up."

Carol's response had been: "I don't feel so much as if I'm growing up—I feel like I'm dying down, or at least getting a kind of spiritual 'middle-aged spread'!" Another friend had urged them to get "re-baptized." "Your problem is that you have a defective foundation." She had been very persuasive, and Bill and Carol were feeling desperate, so they had actually gone with her to her church on a Sunday night, and been duly "dunked." They had both felt refreshed by the experience, and they had reconsecrated themselves, but the refreshing didn't last long. Their feeling about it all was not helped when they discovered that the little church where the "re-baptism" had taken place was engaged in a bitter quarrel over whether baptism in the name of the Trinity would "work," or whether it had to be in the name of Jesus!

"When they decide, I guess they're going to want to do us over!" Bill had commented. "Sort of like calling a car back to the factory to correct a manufacturing error! No, they're sweet people, and they really want to help, but that's not where it's at." And Carol felt the same way.

Carol came out of her reminiscences and glanced at the clock: "Tony! Time to get up!" A muffled response from somewhere in the back of the house signaled an awakening. Carol walked over to the sink, and began to rinse off the breakfast dishes. Why, in the face of all these wonderful experiences, did she still have ups and downs? *And* those bad dreams! Even after the good time last night, she had had a doozy of a nightmare! The big difference, admittedly, was that now when she dreamed she was being chased by a monster or something, she called upon the name of Jesus! She'd never done *that* before! And when she did, everything turned out okay! She smiled to herself—certainly she had made some progress. But why bad dreams at all? And why didn't she feel now like she'd felt last night? Some of her friends said the whole thing was psychological—"Just emotion, kiddo, that's all!"

No, it wasn't like that. She knew what emotion was: laughing, crying, getting upset, or being wildly happy. She had laughed and cried when Jesus came into her life, and she had been tremendously happy in her tears when she had felt the release of the Holy Spirit, but neither experience had been "just emotion." After all, Bill hadn't laughed or cried when he received Jesus although he'd done a lot of both when he felt the joy of the Holy Spirit released in him! But those feelings came from a source deeper than emotion. Emotion doesn't last, but this *had* lasted unbroken for weeks and months—this deep inner awareness that God was real—and with it a joy and peace they'd never dreamed possible. Why should this wonderful awareness fade?

Bill, sitting on the train, pondered the world in his own mental soliloquy. "Excuse me!" He tugged his black briefcase farther under his knees—the rather shapely blonde had almost tripped over it. Bill's gaze followed her down the aisle. "Wow! Pretty nice!" He quickly turned his eyes away from the young lady.

"What kind of a guy am I, anyway? Jesus said something about 'looking after a woman to lust after her,' didn't He? Lord, I don't know why I could feel so right last night and so wrong this morning."

At the next stop, a large and red-faced man took the seat beside Bill. "I'm supposed to try to tell him about Jesus, but I sure don't feel like it!" Bill inwardly confessed.

"Nice day," he ventured at opening a conversation, but his seatmate grumped a barely audible reply and closed his eyes. With an inward sigh of relief, Bill settled back and looked out of the window.

"Christianity is simply the survival of primitive feelings about the world. The idea of a transcendent God who is concerned about us is just a childish throwback. We all want a big sugar daddy in the sky!" The professor rasped on, his unkempt beard wagging. The class didn't look too keen, probably because they'd heard it all before, with a few variations. One student looked alert though— alert and distressed. He was Tony, the Carters' oldest.

"What's the matter, Tony?" the pretty, long-haired brunette said as she took his hand on the way out of Philosophy 1A. "You look miserable! You were really high on the Lord at that prayer meeting last night. What happened?"

"Him!" said Tony curtly, jerking a thumb at Dr. Waldo, who was shuffling papers in preparation for the next class. "He really bugs me. S'pose he's right and we're wrong? How do we *know*? Maybe what we think is an experience of God *is* all emotional and psychological, just like he says. Anyway, he sure does raise a lot of questions I can't answer."

The girl laughed happily, as she twirled around and walked backwards down the hall in front of him. "Well, dear one," she said, "I'd rather be happy believing in Jesus and the Holy Spirit, and experiencing what I'm experiencing, emotional or not, than to be sharing in Professor Waldo's intellectualism and be as miserable as he looks most of the time!" She swung back into stride beside him and took his hand again.

Tony stared at the grey cement as they walked along. "It's all very well for you, Kathy," he said gloomily, "but *my* mind has to have answers."

"I'm glad mine doesn't, then," said Kathy happily, squeezing his hand. "See you tonight? Okay?"

"Okay," said the young man, still downcast. He walked slowly away to his next class.

5

A Timely Visit

Carol, dishes washed and kitchen tidied, was sitting at the table with her Bible open. She wasn't looking at the pages though; she was staring out the window at the sun glinting on the rich green leaves of the big oak tree. She was trying to pray, but on this morning prayer just didn't seem real.

"Lord, where are you? Why don't I feel like praying? You were so close last night," she said, burying her face in her hands.

She was aroused by the soft tone of the doorbell from the back door. "Sue and Bob Jensen! What a nice surprise! What brings you here at this hour? C'mon in and sit down!" Carol was always amazed at Sue, and here she was again: 9:30 A.M., blonde hair tucked under a scarf, no makeup, but still possessing that glow! How did she do it? The newcomers made themselves at home. Carol posed the coffee pot inquiringly. "Have some?"

"Sure," said Sue, taking off her jacket and hanging it over the back of the chair. "How are things over here?"

"Frantic," said Carol briefly, digging flowered cups and saucers out of the cupboard and handing them to her friends.

Bob settled his big frame comfortably in a chair. "We had it straight, honey," he said to his wife, and then to Carol, "It seemed like the Lord told us to come over and see you, so here we are! This is my day off," he explained, as she filled his cup.

"Yup, here we are," said Sue, brightly. "Now tell us all about it."

"Well, it's silly stuff, I guess," Carol began. "Nothing really earthshaking, but, oh, I don't know. Where does the *joy* go to? That's the first question, I suppose." She looked at her smiling friends. "How do you do it?" She opened her hands and shrugged, "How do you keep it?"

Bob chuckled as he put down his cup. "We don't," he said. "Not always. We have our moments, believe me, but we're learning how to handle them."

"*What* are you learning?"

Sue and Bob looked at each other. "Well," Sue said, thoughtfully, "I guess the most important thing we're learning is that we are spirit as well as soul."

Carol looked blank. There was a long pause.

Bob stepped in. "Carol, Sue said she has a soul *and* a spirit," he repeated.

"Yeah, I heard it the first time, but I don't know *what* you're talking about. It sounds very technical. I mean, I'm not up on philosophy and all that."

"In a way, I suppose you might call it technical," said Bob. "But the Lord did give us brains, right?"

Carol nodded. "Guess you're right," she said, "but I don't see how learning such things would help me with my problems. They're really quite simple! Like, how do you keep praising the Lord when you're surrounded by confusion—kids mainly, you know! I love 'em to pieces, but that doesn't make them easy to live with! Then what do you say to a husband who hates his work? I love Bill, too, a whole lot, but he just can't stand that job of his. The office is a real drag for him. He's just great over the weekend, and especially when we go somewhere, like over at your house last night, but on Monday morning, well, he just collapses! Spiritually, I mean. Then there's Tony. He's such a great kid, and you know he accepted Jesus and was baptized in the Spirit, but now he's in college, and even after only one month we can see the change in him. That stuff he's getting, especially in one of his classes, is beginning to erode his faith. Then there's *me*! I plain get frustrated. I love my family and my home, but sometimes I wonder if I shouldn't have gone on with my education. I was really doing well, you know."

Sue nodded. "Interior design was your forte, wasn't it?"

"Uh-huh. I had been accepted at a top school in New York City, but I got married instead. Now sometimes I feel trapped." Carol paused and looked at her friends. "Is that a terrible thing to say?"

Sue was silent a few moments. "No, it isn't. I know what you're talking about, only I was stronger about it than you. I was out for my rights, long before 'women's lib.' "

"I can't quite feature you as a 'libber.' " Carol looked at her friend with a smile.

"That was some time before you knew me. The Lord really swung me around. Oh, I'm still for women's rights, when they're reasonable and in keeping with God's ideas, but my ornery attitude is gone." She paused and smiled thoughtfully, "Anyway, I went to college, got a degree,

25

and promptly got married!" She gave Bob a loving look.

Bob grinned back and patted her hand, "Sure glad you did!"

"Look," Bob continued, leaning back in his chair, "why don't we stop being mysterious and explain to you what we *are* talking about? Let's see, you're having trouble with your feelings, right?"

Carol nodded.

"And Tony's having a struggle with his intellect?"

"Yup."

"And you and Bill, well, I think you're both battling with decisions and frustrations—he about his job, and you about the career you didn't have, and the family you *do* have!"

"Right on."

"Of course, I'm sure *you* also have your intellectual hang-ups, too, as I'm sure Bill has problems with his feelings, and Tony with frustrations, and so forth."

"What are you driving at?" Carol moved her chair a little closer, and leaned forward attentively.

6

An Important Difference

"Well, don't you see that your problems are all with your emotions, your intellect, and your will?" Bob continued.

"Isn't that about all there is?" Carol shrugged and laughed.

Sue shook her head emphatically and picked up the discussion. "Oh, no," she said. "Those are all a part of your soul. If that's all there was, you'd be somewhat in the same class as Snowball there." She nodded toward the Carters' large white Persian sleeping on the windowsill. "She's got intellect, right?"

Carol laughed again. "She sure has. More than she lets on, I think. She almost outsmarts me sometimes!"

"And she's got emotions?" Sue continued.

"No question about that!"

"What about *will*?"

"I should estimate about 99 percent will, or maybe *won't!*"

"Then Snowball certainly has a soul—a psychological

nature?"

Carol said nothing, but looked thoughtful.

"Okay, then," Bob joined back in, "what's the difference between you and her?"

Carol ruffled her brow. "Well, I'm not sure—except she's *furrier* than I am," she offered, laughing.

"Well, *are* you just an animal?" Sue inquired further, laughing too.

"At college they said I was—kind of a super-animal, you know; evolved more, and all that sort of thing. Primates. That's what our minister says too. He believes God created us by developing us from the lower animals."

"Well, supposing it were true, isn't there still something special about a human being?"

Carol nodded slowly. "Uh-huh. Our minister says God kind of put something extra into this super-animal at a certain point and that's what makes us different from other animals."

"Okay. Whether you believe man's body evolved out of lower forms of life, or God made man separately from the animals, there *is* something basically different about him, isn't there?"

"Go on."

"You're asking how to keep your joy in the Lord, right?"

Carol nodded wistfully.

"Well, when you feel that kind of happiness, you know it's a lot deeper than emotional excitement, don't you?"

"Sure do. I could get myself worked up, but that's not what I'm looking for."

"Well, that deep joy comes from your spirit, where your new life is ever since you accepted Jesus and the Holy Spirit came to live in you. But emotions come from your soul.''

"I always thought soul and spirit were the same thing, just two different terms." Carol gestured with her spoon.

"They are part of *one* person, namely you," Bob replied. "But, you see, if you think of your soul and your spirit as the same thing—that is, if you think you only have a body and a soul—or whatever you choose to call these two parts, you're open to confusion in several ways. You know you were supposed to have been born again of the Holy Spirit when you received Jesus. You've been told you are therefore a new creature. Obviously that new creature must be in the spiritual part of you. Now, if you act in a way that isn't right, or talk that way, or even feel that way, you're likely to ask yourself: 'What's the matter with me? I thought I was supposed to be a new creature. How come I could have thoughts like I'm having, or do and say the things I do? I guess I didn't really get reborn of the Spirit, or if I did, I lost it!' "

"Yeah, I see what you mean."

"Because they do not recognize the difference between soul and spirit, various groups of Christians deal with this problem in different ways," Bob went on. "The Catholic tradition teaches that there is 'venial' sin which a person can commit and not lose his salvation, and 'mortal' sin which destroys one's relationship with God, in which case the person must confess and be forgiven before he can once more be in a 'state of grace.'

"Among Protestants," Bob continued, "the belief has moved all the way from those who taught there was no way for a person to lose out—'once in grace, always in grace'—and those who felt that even a very small misdeed would cause them to be 'backslidden,' so they must go back to the altar and get saved all over again. It's the same idea."

"But," said Carol, frowning slightly, "aren't there ways a person can lose salvation? I mean, are you saying, 'Once saved, always saved'? Is that where you are?"

"No," said Bob, "I'm not trying to say that, although I'd rather be there than at the other extreme. If a person really renounced Jesus, and truly wanted Him to leave, he might succeed in driving Him away. Even that is doubtful ground, though, because He loves us far more than we love Him. At any rate, He isn't going to leave us just because we don't always act and speak and think the way He wants us to."

"Is that why," put in Carol, "some people are always running around trying to find the right church? They feel there must be something wrong with their salvation— they didn't quite get it right, otherwise they wouldn't still be doing bad things?"

"On the other hand," Sue joined in, "the person may decide that his or her *body* is the big problem. Their spiritual part is supposed to be in tune with the Lord, but they don't feel that way, so they blame their physical part, and may go through all kinds of things—giving up food, marital relations, anything that encourages what they think of as the wicked body."

"Excuse me for interrupting," Carol began, "but do you know that's exactly what Maisie Colton is doing? She's decided she can't possibly stay spiritual while she's still having physical relations with her hubby, so she's decided to sleep alone!"

"Uh-huh," nodded Sue, "and pretty miserable she looks, too, and her husband looks worse. It's odd, because you'd think Paul the apostle settled that issue long ago when he said not to deprive one another of normal relations.[1] Then, of course, there's eating and drinking. We knew a chap who fasted on water forty days, in order to get really 'spiritual.' Nearly killed himself, too!"

"That's why people have lain on beds of nails and worn hair shirts, and scourged themselves, trying to 'tame' the body, yet it's all wide of the mark, because the body itself is innocent," said Bob.

"I don't know about *that!* Don't our physical drives get us into trouble?"

"No, it isn't our physical drives that are bad," said Bob. "It's what we decide to do with them. It's the kind of orders we give our bodies—the control we have over them that steers them in the right or wrong direction. It was Paul, again, who said that he kept his body 'under'—meaning, of course, 'under control.' I got a traffic ticket the other day," Bob continued. "I was going thirty miles in a twenty-mile zone. I didn't say to the officer, 'But officer, I didn't do it! It was my car that did it!' "

Carol laughed. "No, I guess that wouldn't have gone down too well."

"I heard a story," said Sue, "about a man who was trying to ride a donkey. The donkey kicked and kicked, and finally succeeded in getting a hoof in one of the stirrups. The man looked down and said to the donkey: 'If you're going to get on, I'm going to get off!' "

"Well said!" Bob laughed. "We mustn't let the body get into the driver's seat, or the donkey in the saddle either! We *can* control our physical drives—whether we are going to act by our own decisions, or whether we are just going to react to the stimuli applied to our bodies. I mean, you can be very hungry, and just sitting down to a good dinner, but if a starving man rings your doorbell, you'd give him your dinner in spite of your physical drives, right?"

[1] 1 Corinthians 7:3-5.

31

"Yes, I would. I might not *want* to, though," Carol added frankly.

"That's because your soul would rule the desires of your body. You see," Bob went on, "more and more we realize how much depends on what we *decide* to do. Psychologists are coming to realize that even in some advanced forms of insanity, the person is *choosing* his condition."

Carol waved her hands despairingly. "Hold it! Hold it! This 'soul and spirit' thing, you haven't explained what you mean. I'm still not with you."

"Sorry," said Bob. "Lots of people have been confused on this. Many great thinkers and theologians have failed to see it but today the Holy Spirit really seems to be underlining it. Did you ever read 1 Thessalonians 5:23? 'I pray God your whole *spirit* and *soul* and *body* be preserved blameless unto the coming of our Lord Jesus Christ'?"

"Oh," said Carol. She thought a moment. "Hey, in that—that, uh, Magnifi-something-or-other you say in your church. What Jesus' mother, Mary, said, you know? I used to like it when I went to chapel at college sometimes. It's real pretty—oh, I remember: 'My *soul* doth magnify the Lord, and my *spirit* hath rejoiced in God my Savior.' Is *that* what you're talking about?"

"The Magnificat. Good for you!" said Sue. "I hadn't thought of that. Yes, Mary seemed to know the difference between her soul and spirit.[2] That's the way we should be, our souls and spirits rejoicing and magnifying God. Our previous minister used to tell us it was just Hebrew poetry, repeating a thought, but we think we know better now! Anyway, you get the idea."

Carol raised her eyebrows. "Hey, that's great! I'm going to hunt up some other references."

---

[2]Luke 1:46, 47. The Greek reads: "My soul (*psuche*) magnifies the Lord, and my spirit (*pneuma*) exults in God my Savior."

7

Why Can't We Stay Free?

"Did you ever notice in the Bible that someone will say things like: 'Why are you in despair, O my soul?' or 'Praise the Lord, O my soul!'?"

Carol thought about this a minute, then reached for a Bible on the sideboard. "Where's that passage you just quoted?" she asked.

"Psalm 42."

"One of these new versions," explained Carol, turning the pages. "I have trouble with the 'thees' and 'thous' in the old one."

"I know what you mean," said Sue, "I love the old King James Version. In fact, it's one of the most accurate on soul and spirit, but the new ones sure are easier to read. I use them all."

Carol was hunting for the verse. "Here it is," she announced. "Psalm 42:5: 'Why are you in despair, O my soul? And why have you become disturbed within me? Hope in God, for I shall yet praise Him, for the help of His presence.' Oh, and here it is again in the eleventh verse, and in the *next* Psalm, too! Boy, God must have wanted us to get the point, huh?'' She paused a moment, then added, 'Y'know it's kind of encouraging to know that King David, or whoever wrote that Psalm, had some problems, too! I think I begin to get it. If I have a spirit and a soul, then, like David, I could be having trouble in my soul, even though I've come alive spiritually.''

Bob smiled. "You're getting the idea," he said. "And David did get in trouble you remember. A kid once wrote on a Bible exam: 'If David had any problem it was a slight tendency to adultery!' ''

"Well, that's no joke, either," said Carol. "I know at least one gal who accepted Jesus, was baptized in the Holy Spirit, and now she's in a real mess: drugs, alcohol, divorced from her husband, got pregnant, and just had an abortion. Is that because of a *soul* problem?"

Bob nodded vigorously, "Only too true," he agreed. "Probably the thing that has kept more people from accepting the release or baptism in the Holy Spirit in their lives is the false idea that it makes the person perfectly holy," he snapped his fingers, "just like that. Why, I've acted worse in some ways since I was baptized in the Holy Spirit than before."

Carol looked startled. "You?" she said. "Problems?"

Bob leaned back and roared with laughter. "Carol," he said, "don't do that to me! You're making the same mistake I do sometimes. I go to a meeting and listen to a speaker tell about all the victories and triumphs in his or her life, and I think, 'Boy, it must be great not to have any problems—to just sail along in the power of the Lord all the time!' But you know something, that kind of thinking has led to lots of trouble. That's why Jesus told us not to call anyone on earth 'father,' or 'teacher,' or 'master.' He wasn't talking about titles. It's okay to keep on calling your daddy 'father,' or for me to call my priest 'father.' It's okay for me or Bill to accept the title of 'mister,' which is a weakened form of 'master.' Jesus really meant, 'Don't be anyone's disciple, except mine. Don't be a follower of men.' "

Carol still looked a little disturbed. "But *what* kind of problems do you have, Bob?" she asked, very seriously. "I mean, can you tell me?"

"Well, my most difficult problem has been with my temper. I always called it being a 'high-power' person. You know, 'short-fused'! It came out mostly in the form of impatience, but every once in a while I'd blow up. Ask Sue."

"He's telling you like it is," said his wife with a smile.

"And I want you to know, Carol, that I've never had so much trouble with that bad temper as I did *after* I was baptized in the Holy Spirit!"

"Why is that?"

"Well, you see, although I didn't let my temper fly very often, I was really keeping a dangerous wild animal inside me. I kept it chained most of the time so I didn't realize how dangerous it was, and neither did anyone else. But as the Holy Spirit began to free my emotions, He unchained the critter I was nurturing. It made me at least *begin* to co-operate with the Lord in doing something about it."

Sue picked up on the topic. "It isn't just moral problems, or emotional problems," she said. "People who have received the release of the Holy Spirit are more sensitive and can get into other kinds of difficulties if they don't learn to walk in the Spirit. I was just a little startled when I found that one of my good 'Spirit-filled' friends had joined a weird religious cult, and another was experimenting with Transcendental Meditation!"

"Those are intellectual tangles, although they lead quickly into spiritual ones. Take a look at Hebrews 4:12 while you're at it," said Bob, sliding the Bible to his side of the table. "Here, let me read it to you: 'The Word of God is living and powerful, and sharper than a two-edged sword, even dividing the soul and the spirit. . . .' "

"Oh," said Carol. "I see. I'd wondered about that verse. There are a lot of things that go on in the soul that get blamed on the spirit, right?"

"Right," agreed Bob. "Understanding the difference between these two areas helps you to learn to 'walk in the spirit' so that the soul can be healed and corrected. The Bible often refers to 'walking in the spirit,' it never tells us to 'walk in the soul,' or to live by the dictates of the soul. Though it isn't always easy to divide between the soul and the spirit, I can promise you, if you let Jesus—who is Himself the Word of God—show you how it'll help you stay free and joyful. It'll help you see where your problems are, and know what to do about them."

Carol looked puzzled again. "But Bob, are we divided into parts? I mean, going back to David, if his spirit was speaking to his soul, does that mean there are sort of two people inside him, and one can talk to the other? We are all in one piece, aren't we?"

Bob nodded. "Good thinking. No, it isn't David's spirit speaking to his soul, it's rather that David himself is letting his spirit take authority over his soul."

Carol looked at Bob and Sue thoughtfully. "I'll bet there's a lot more to be said about all this, isn't there?"

"Right you are." Bob paused a moment, then took a pen out of his shirt pocket. "Got a piece of paper?" he asked. "I want to draw you a picture."

* * *

Perhaps even though you've accepted Jesus and the power of the Holy Spirit, you have some of the same questions Bill and Carol had. Maybe you've said something like: "If I can feel so close to God sometimes, and see Him do wonderful things, how can I still at other times feel depressed and out of it?" Perhaps you still have problems like Bill Carter, not liking your job, or eyeing the girls. Or Carol, frustrated with homemaking and an unrealized career, or Tony, with intellectual doubts. Maybe you've wondered, "How *can* a Christian say some of the things I say, think some of the things I think, or do some of the things I do? *Why* do I still mess up far too often? Am I backslidden? Have I lost out with the Lord?"

For now, let's leave the Carters and Jensens to their discussion and talk directly. There *is* a lot more to be said. We'll show you, in a minute, the picture Bob drew for Carol, and some other diagrams. These were life-changing insights for Bob and Sue; they were for us, and they can be for you.

When you first receive Jesus, and your spirit comes alive in the Holy Spirit, it's a wonderful day, and life looks different.

> "Heaven above is softer blue,
> Earth around is sweeter green;
> Something lives in every hue
> Christless eyes have never seen. . . .
> (George Robinson, "I Am His and He Is Mine")

But as the days go by, the thrill of that first encounter tends to weaken, and although you don't forget it, the immediate experience drops into the background.

37

Then, if you have received the baptism in the Holy Spirit, you have probably experienced freedom and joy and reality you hadn't dreamed possible. But are you now as filled with the joy in the Holy Spirit as you were? You've heard it said that people should be locked up for the first six months after they are baptized in the Spirit because they are so joyful and aware of the Lord that they don't always use wisdom. But maybe the more experienced Christians say this in part because they are envious of the beginner's freedom, and wish they were still as excited about it all as they were in *their* first six months.

We talk about maturing, but do we mean, as Carol said, a kind of "middle-aged spread"? We're not saying we don't need wisdom, but does that necessitate losing power and freedom? Maybe you are different. Maybe you have none of these problems. But for most of us, the difficult question seems to be, "How do you keep on keeping on?"

What works against freedom in the Spirit? How can you learn to keep free? For us, one concept that helps so much is realizing that we are not two-part creatures, but three-part beings—that in our bodies live both a soul and spirit. And when the soul functions on its own, it quenches the freedom of the Holy Spirit who is living in our spirits, so that He cannot work in our souls the way He wants to.

8

You Must Understand Yourself

Unless you understand some basics about yourself you can start off with a roar in the Spirit, only to get sidetracked or discouraged en route. Our potential can be frittered away in a maze of personal "hang-ups," or we can go wrong doctrinally or morally. Satan fights hard to keep God's power from *continuing* to flow in God's people. He isn't too concerned when believers reminisce about what happened years ago, or even last year, just so long as they think: "These things are not for *today*."

You know what a "yo-yo Christian" is, don't you? One who has lots of ups and downs! Oh, yes, *we* have them too. "What?", you may ask, "you Christian leaders and authors have ups and downs?" Yes, we're human, but understanding the difference between soul and spirit is helping us become steadier. We want to tell you some of the things we've found out. They'll be helpful to you, we're sure.

We wish we could be talking to you in person, and drawing some pictures on the blackboard. Since we can't, please imagine we are, and let the drawings in this book be the blackboard.

Let's start by asking a question: Have you always thought of yourself as twofold? Most people, Christians included, would say: "I have a soul and a body." Some would probably say, "I have a mind and a body," but it amounts to the same thing; there are two parts, the inner self and the outer self. After all, it seems pretty clear that there are two worlds, the material and the spiritual. The material world includes all the things you can touch and see. The spiritual one includes things like mind, thought, feelings, and/or anything that has to do with God, or other "spiritual" beings. Our physical bodies obviously belong to the material realm and our souls or spirits to the spiritual world.

This was our picture, too, until we discovered something very important was being left out.

What God Says About Us

Anthropology is the study of human beings and their cultures. In the courses some of you took in college you were probably told that human beings are the emerging product of blind chance—"a gruesome accident," as one great physicist put it. But we need to know what the maker says about the product. "When all else fails," goes the saying, "read the instruction book." What does the Manufacturer's Handbook (as Harold Hill calls the Bible) have to say about it? What does *God* say about us?

The Book of Genesis tells very briefly about God making the world and the things in it. It isn't meant to be a scientific treatise, but it gives the basic facts in vivid picture. God makes the world, and separates the earth from the water, then He directs the earth to produce vegetable life. Next He tells the water to bring forth all kinds of aquatic life and birds.[1] God turns to the earth again, and commands it to produce all kinds of animals. Note each time God had put the potential there, and now He orders the water and earth to respond as He has made them able to do (Gen. 1:11, 24).

But then comes a pause in the record; God says, "Let us make man in our image, after our likeness. . . . So God made man of the dust of the earth, and breathed into his nostrils the breath of life, and man became a living soul" (Gen. 1:26; 2:7). God does not command the earth to "bring forth" human beings, He creates them by a special and separate action.

"Back in 1961," says Rita, "I had just been wonderfully renewed in my own experience of God. I had gone to work for the state of Florida in the welfare department, and was coming into frequent contact with the messes people sometimes make of their lives.

"My cases went something like this:

1. Mother and father attempt to give away their baby at a local tavern.
2. Woman whose alcoholic husband is in jail, is living with another man, twenty years her junior. He beat her with a Coke bottle wrapped in a towel. Her four children are in foster homes.
3. Teen-age girl in solitary confinement at detention home after slashing her wrists. She comes from well-to-do home, but says she receives no love there.

"Those first months on the job had me thinking, sometimes into the wee hours, about people with such great problems and extreme behavior. At a behavioral science

---

[1]Birds? Out of the water? Once again the Bible is accurate. Modern investigators claim that birds are descendants of reptiles that lived in the water.

seminar one evening, the lecturer convincingly argued that man is nothing more than an animal. His words disturbed me because they were seemingly confirmed by my current experience, yet still they didn't seem right. For one thing, no animal would act like some of my charges did! I went to sleep that night with the question on my mind, and when I woke in the morning it seemed as though God said to me clearly: *I am a Triune God, and you are made in My image; how then could you be animal?* It was a simple answer, yet profound, and launched me into a search to understand what it meant for man to be triune, threefold, like God."

Human Beings Are Different

God joined spirit, which was like Him, with material stuff, "dust of the earth," and made something new, a human being. We don't know what kind of creatures God may have made in the far-flung reaches of this universe, or of other worlds He may have created, in other dimensions unthinkable to us, but we know that on this earth, when God made human beings He was making creatures that would bridge between the spiritual and material worlds.

Let's draw a diagram. Genesis says that God breathed spirit into matter, and "man became a living soul." So now, in addition to two dimensions, spiritual and physical, we have another, the soul or psychological dimension.

The newly created spirit that came down from God into "the dust of the earth" (Gen. 2), was *not* God's own Spirit, but a spirit made *like* Him. "God made man in his *image*" (Gen. 1:27). "The Lord . . . formed the spirit of man within him" (Zech. 12:1, see also Heb. 12:9). If our spirits were just little pieces of God's Spirit, we wouldn't be individual people distinct from God, we'd be sort of

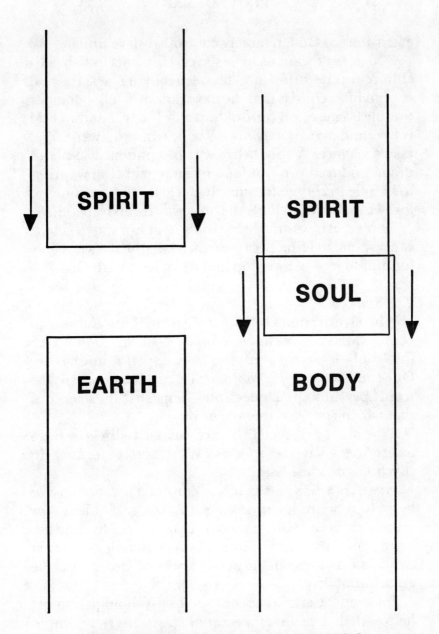

GOD CREATES HUMAN BEINGS

extensions of God, remotely controlled slave units.

God doesn't want us to be slaves. He wants us to be His children. The difference between buying a slave and conceiving a child is that the slave cannot disobey or make trouble because you control him absolutely, but the child is free, and may or may not do or be what you want. You take a chance. A robot that was programmed to act as though it loved you wouldn't mean much! God wants us to be able to choose for ourselves whether we're going to love Him, because that's the only way it can be real love.

Man's spirit was made in God's image or likeness so it can respond to Him. Because man has a spirit, it's possible for him to have fellowship and friendship with God.

The Soul

When spirit comes into matter a third thing comes into being. "Man became a living *soul*" (Gen. 2:7). The Greek for "soul" is *psuche*, "psyche" as we spell it in English. Our souls are our *psycho*logical part. That's where the word "psychology" comes from—it means "the science of that which concerns the *psyche* or soul."

As a matter of fact this gives us an indirect way to determine what the soul is. What sort of things do psychologists deal with?

Intellect? Yes, a person might consult a psychologist to help him with his thinking. A college student, for example, might talk to a counselor to help him or her learn how to study properly. A psychologist often administers tests of general aptitude to determine academic ability.

Emotions? Certainly people go to psychologists to get help with their feelings or emotions: fear, anger, rejection, etc.

Will? Yes, psychology is concerned with the *will*, how to become motivated, how to deal with frustration and conflict, how to plan.

The intellect involves the way we think; the will involves decision making; the emotions concern what we feel. The soul is the *ego*, the psychological nature, the center of personality. It's what we see and know about one another. Whether we're inhibited or boisterous, highly educated or average, psychologically whole or damaged. It's a trinity within a trinity.

Right now let's settle a question Carol asked. You may be asking it as well. We aren't saying that a human being is all divided up into pieces! When we talk of the spirit, soul, and body, and then of the three parts of the soul, it's like describing the house you live in. It is one house, but it has many rooms, and in the rooms there are different pieces of furniture. Your kitchen or bedroom is a very definite place in your house, serving a specific purpose, but no room in your house could exist on its own; it's just a part of the house.

The Body

The body is the physical equipment by which the spirit and soul contact the material universe. It receives *im*pressions; that is, the information that comes in from the physical world and is passed along to the soul. The impressions come through the "senses": touching, tasting, smelling, hearing, seeing. Some investigators say we may have as many as twenty-six distinguishable senses, however, including such things as balance, our sense of orientation in the spatial world around us, the kinetic sense (which enables you to touch the tip of your

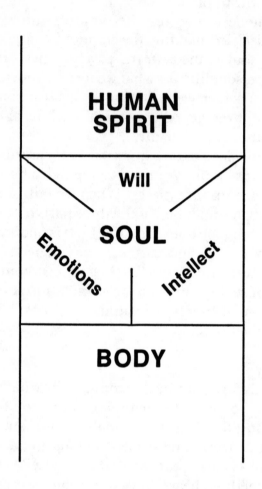

A TRINITY WITHIN A TRINITY

nose in the dark), etc.

The body influences the world around by *ex*pression. There are many ways in which we express ourselves, but we may sum them up as "hands," the things we *do;* "feet," the places we *go;* and "voice," the things we *say.*

The human spirit in fellowship with God, spirit inspiring soul, and soul ruling body—that's how human beings were intended to function. Here is the bridge between the spiritual world and the physical earth. God wanted to have a creature that was adapted to living on the earth, and at the same time would be in fellowship with Him in the Spirit. Not a slave, but a free agent who would be God's representative on the earth. He or she would have power and authority to rule the earth, take care of it, and the other creatures on it, and make it a more beautiful and wonderful place (Gen. 1:26-28; 2:15).

Human beings were meant to enjoy both the beauty of earth, and the pleasure of physical life on it, and at the same time to be enjoying God, and the glories of His heavenly kingdom. They were to be ways by which God's glory could be seen on the earth, because they were made in His image, and so would think, speak and act like Him.

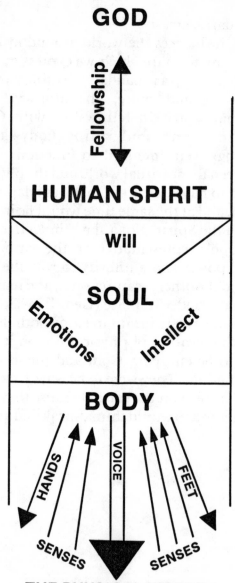

HOW GOD MEANT US TO FUNCTION

48

9

The Great Disaster

We painted a nice picture in the preceding chapter, but if humanity started off that way, something's gone wrong. There isn't much evidence that human beings are living in fellowship with God. In fact, a good proportion of the human race doesn't seem to think He exists at all. The strongest political system in the world today is built on the conviction that there is no God. Even in the USA it is unlawful to bring God officially into government or education. In fact, it's considered bad taste to talk about Him publicly at all, except in church, and even in many churches you've got to be a little careful!

Then, too, you would hardly think, from the record of human history, that mankind had been in touch with or guided by a loving God. The story, right to the present, is one long record of violence, cruelty and selfishness, what Bobby Burns called "man's inhumanity to man."

Most would still agree that Jesus Christ was the greatest and best person who ever lived, and many believe He was personally God, yet when He came to this planet, people were not very friendly—they nailed Him to a cross.

The Problem of Evil

Philosophers struggle with the "problem of evil." "If God is good, and He made the world, where did bad things come from?" Christians answer that God gave genuine freedom to some of the creatures He made, in order to have friendship with them, and share love with them. They could *choose* to break fellowship and refuse love, to turn against God, and some of them did. The basis of all evil is this broken fellowship. Evil originates in the wrong use of freedom.

God created people free to make up their own minds. He wanted them to choose to love and follow Him. They decided there was something they were missing, that God was holding out on them, so to speak, and so determined to "do their own thing."

Why didn't God protect them against this? Remember what we've been saying about free will, and what God wanted from human beings? He wanted them to love Him freely, which is the only way you can love anyone. Therefore He could not protect them from the temptation *not* to love Him. Human beings had to learn by experience.

There is no other way. If a man is in love with a girl, he cannot protect against the possibility that she might "fall" for someone else. She has to make up her own mind. Remember the old fairy tales in which the wicked suitor locks the beautiful princess in a tower to prevent any other lover from reaching her? If somebody really did this to his lady love, he might succeed in keeping her outwardly faithful, but he would always have the uneasy feeling that *if* his intended had the chance she just *might* be untrue!

50

The third chapter of the Book of Genesis gives a picture of what happened to the first humans. The man and the woman, just created, are living happily in the Garden of Eden. God is their friend. He comes and "walks in the garden in the cool of the day." They have perfect spirits, souls and bodies. They don't know anything about intellectual doubts, emotional upsets, or struggles with frustration and ambition. They don't know anything about sickness or death. They have "heaven on earth." Their lives are simply joyful, peaceful and loving. They don't have to strain to make a living. Everything they need is provided. Everything they do is done "for fun." They don't know anything about "oughts" and "shoulds." They don't know what it is to be tired or bored. Everything that happens is fresh and new. What a life!

Yet they "blew" it!

Rebellion Was Afoot

It might not have happened if they had not been influenced by a rebellion which was already afoot in the universe. When God first began to create the heavens and the earth, because He wanted to share His joy, He created powerful spiritual beings to work with Him. We call them "angels." This often brings to mind a picture of a winged creature of indeterminate gender, probably with long blond curls, dressed in a white gown, looking sentimental, or perhaps looking pained, if not actually depressed!

Nothing could be farther from the biblical picture of an angel. The angels in the Bible are always depicted as powerful masculine beings, in fact, sometimes they are called "men" (i.e., Acts 1:10). When they show up, the first thing they say is: "Don't be afraid," and with reason! The angel on the Day of Resurrection had a face "like lightning"! When he landed, he caused an earthquake, and so scared the tough soldiers who were guarding the tomb where Jesus was that they passed out cold (Matt. 28:2-4)! They had a free will too. They were and are persons, although they don't have bodies like ours. (Apparently they can appear in the form of human beings, at least the angels and archangels can.) One of the highest of these beings used his freedom to start a rebellion against God; he became consumed with the idea of making himself equal to God. When he broke fellowship with God, he lost all meaning for his own existence, and only wanted to spoil everything God was doing.[1]

In the Beginning

In the Genesis story the enemy comes masquerading as a serpent. It may seem strange to us that Mother Eve would want to talk with this creature at all but the Scripture says that he was the most "subtil" of the animals—clever and crafty. Since part of his punishment later on was that he would crawl on his belly, presumably at this time he was equipped with legs, and must have been an attractive and intelligent being.

This creature corners Mother Eve and says to her in effect, "Why are you letting God keep you down? Don't you know you could launch out on your own, and then you'd be just like God, able to run your own life?" He didn't at first try to get Adam and Eve to hate or reject God completely, but just to turn away from total dependence on Him, and go "into business for themselves," so to speak (Gen. 3:1-5).

[1]People ask, "Why did God create Satan at all?" God didn't create Satan. God created Lucifer, a great angelic power, whose name means "shining one." He rebelled against God, and so became Satan, the prince of darkness.

And they fell for the line. They believed the serpent when he pointed out that God was perhaps not leveling with them, but trying to keep them down, and that they should declare their "rights." So they asserted their independence by partaking of the "tree of the knowledge of good and evil."

When they did this, they were really saying to God, "We don't trust you. We don't believe you mean the best for us, and so we're going to step out on our own and see what we can do for ourselves." But if you say to a friend, "I don't trust you," the friendship is broken right there, because mutual trust is essential to friendship. Not only that, but there is no way for the friend to renew the friendship from his side, no matter how much he may want to, because *you* don't trust *him*. A mediator, a go-between, is needed.

The first humans thought they could back away from God just far enough to run their own lives, getting a little help from Him when they needed it, but not having to trust Him totally, and without His "interfering" in their plans. They were saying to God, "Don't call us, we'll call you!" But in those days, once the fellowship was broken, there was no mediator, no way to bridge the gap. God Himself could not bring them back to Him without taking away their freedom, making puppets out of them.

They had thought they would be independent operators, but their dream was rudely shattered, for they had further underestimated the situation. They had thought to claim neutrality, so that they could "do their own thing," but when they turned their backs on God, they were immediately claimed by Satan, whom they had chosen to obey. God had given the humans authority over the earth. The enemy now claimed that authority, and became what Jesus Himself called, "the prince of this world" (John 14:30).

(He is also called "Satan" which means the "adversary" or "opponent," or "the devil," from Greek, *diabolos*, which means a "slanderer.")

This was still not the end of the catastrophe, because when Satan gained authority over the earth, he immediately let in a flood of other evil beings: fallen spiritual powers who had joined him in his rebellion, and demon spirits of all kinds. The humans not only found themselves cut off from spiritual fellowship with God, but living in a world that was flooded with spiritual darkness, under the domination of Satan, and surrounded by all kinds of evil spiritual entities. So Paul writes, "Our struggle isn't with flesh and blood, but with archons, authorities, with the world-rulers of the darkness of this age, with spiritual powers of wickedness in the heavenlies" (Eph. 6:12, literal). Earth had become occupied territory.

In tempting Mother Eve and Father Adam, the serpent appealed to their physical nature; the fruit was "good for food." He appealed to their emotions; it was "pleasant to the eyes," aesthetically appealing. To their wills, "it was to be *desired* to make one wise." To the intellect, "You will be as gods, knowing good and evil." Thus he tempted their souls and their bodies.

However, he had not yet tried to tempt them spiritually; that is, he had kept his identity a secret and not tried to get them to commit themselves to him personally, to worship him as a god. That would have been his next move, to invade and take over their spirits. They would then have been hopelessly in his power, not just in body and soul, but in spirit, too, totally possessed. For their own protection, therefore, God closed off their spirits.

Man's Spirit Closed to God Too
When God did this, of course, He not only shut the enemy

out, but He shut Himself out. The humans were not open to any spiritual relationship, good or bad. Their spirits went dark and became useless and pointless.

We might compare this to a submarine that is disabled and lying on the sea bottom. The rescue crew cannot just open the hatch and go into the vessel, because they would let in the water which surrounds it at tremendous pressure. So God cannot open the door of man's spirit, for in so doing He would make it possible for the powers of darkness to come in. Some special arrangement is needed that would reach down to the submarine from the world above the water. The same is true for fallen man. The door of man's spirit cannot be opened until it can in some way be opened to the world above the darkness.

In Genesis, after Adam and Eve rejected God, God closed the Garden of Eden to them and placed cherubim and a flaming sword to guard the way to the tree of life. This is symbolic of God's closing off the human spirit.

God Himself *cannot* reach the human race through the spiritual door because He Himself closed it for man's protection. Before it can be opened again, something must be done to protect human beings from the forces of evil that surround them.

Wandering in the Dark

What was the condition of human beings after fellowship with God was broken? First, they had no spiritual reference. That means they were *lost*. Right? If you don't know who you are, or where you're going, you're lost—and that's exactly what the word means when we talk about "lost souls." A person can be a "jolly good fellow" or a "real good gal," kind, friendly, lots of fun, a good neighbor, a good sport, etc., etc., and still be a "lost soul," not knowing who they are, or where they are going.

Dennis likes to tell a story about his early flight training: "I was with my instructor in a little Cherokee 160 flying over the Seattle area. My instructor, a very definite guy, as all good instructors should be, asked, 'Where are we?' What a question! Here I had the aircraft straight and level and on a fairly consistent altitude, and he wants to know where we are! I gave an honest answer (I had no choice!) and I said, 'I don't know.' Whereupon my instructor friend became just a tad sarcastic and replied, 'That's great. We're making good time, but we're lost.'

"What a terrific illustration of the human predicament," says Dennis. "We're making good time. We can travel above the speed of sound, and even break away from the gravity of earth to circle the moon. Human beings have all kinds of efficient ways of getting places, but ultimately don't know where they're going, or even where they *are*, or why."

God had warned Adam that if he disobeyed he would die, yet Adam's soul and body lived 930 years after his disobedience. Nevertheless, his *spirit* died to God, on the day he broke the fellowship.

Notice that the tree of life was not forbidden to them before (Gen. 2:16, 17). This means that Adam and Eve were not designed to die. Their lives could have been maintained indefinitely by God's direct power, but now such an extension of their lives would be simply perpetuating their misery. Death became a necessity, the only door by which they could hope to escape from Satan. This is why the Scripture says many times that death came into the world because of sin (Rom. 5:12, 17, 21; 1 Cor. 15:21, 56, et al.) and that "the wages of sin is death" (Rom. 6:23).

Since the spirit could no longer give guidance, the soul took over. The intellect said, "*I'll* figure it out. I'll *think* my way through. Just get me a little more information."

The *will* says: "If we can just *try* a little harder, everything will be all right. The important thing is to find some rules and start keeping them. The main thing is to be sincere, and determined, and make an effort."

The *emotions* say: "Whatever makes you happy and helps you feel good must be the way to go." But none of the three really know where they are going, so the result is confusion. And this is precisely the situation with the people you and I meet day by day as we go about our business in the world. You can tell they're lost by looking in their eyes. They don't know who they are or where they're going. And they are trying to guide themselves by thinking, willing, and feeling—what else is there, if you're not in touch with God?

Dennis says again: "We can continue with our aviation illustration. At a busy airport there may be dozens of airplanes wanting to take off, land, or just fly through the airspace. They don't normally collide with one another. Why? Because they are all in communication with the air traffic control facilities—Approach Control, Departure Control, the Tower, Ground Control, etc.—and because the guy or gal on the ground knows where the airplanes are, he or she can tell the pilots where it's safe to fly, and when it is safe to approach and land, or take off and go. There is order and safety around the air terminal because everyone is under 'positive control.' "

When the human race lost contact with God, they became like aircraft who are out of touch with the controller, and they soon began bumping into one another. This would be bad enough, but add to it the fact that the pilots of the various airplanes are not only lost and confused, but angry and rebellious, and the stage is set for some real trouble.

The first human pair had children, and passed their spiritual deadness along to them. They, in turn, had families and the earth began to be populated. This is what God had meant to happen, but of course He had meant them all to know and love Him, and to let Him guide them and protect them. Now they were wandering in the dark, rebellious against God, and filled with themselves.

They soon began to hurt one another. The first bloodshed occurred when Adam and Eve's first son, Cain, murdered his brother, Abel (Gen. 4). This kind of thing grew more and more common until in Genesis 6 it says that "All the earth was filled with violence." You see, it wasn't only that people didn't know where they were going, hurting one another in the confusion—like people stampeding out of a burning building. They began to hurt one another now, not just from confusion, but from active hatred.

Remember, too, that they were surrounded by forces of spiritual evil, actively *tempting* mankind, trying to pull them farther away from God, and human beings became more and more angry and rebellious as the influence of the enemy gained on them. Satan couldn't reach the human spirits directly because God had closed the door, but he could harass their intellects, wills, and emotions, and their bodies too.

People Forgot What God Was Like
People quickly forgot what God was really like, which made it easier for the enemy to get them to follow him. They were closed to him spiritually but he hoped to reach in through their bodies and souls, through the things he

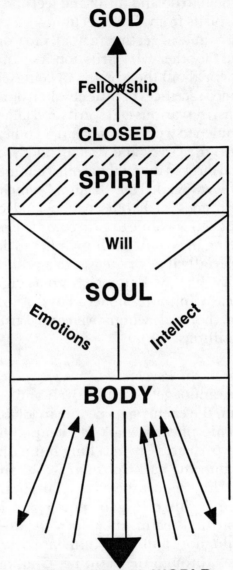

GOD

Fellowship

CLOSED

SPIRIT

Will

SOUL

Emotions   Intellect

BODY

THE PHYSICAL WORLD
BROKEN FELLOWSHIP AND CLOSED SPIRIT

would get them to do and think and feel and will, and so reach their spirits from that direction.

Soon he was able to get them actually to worship him as a "god," and the other evil spirits, too. You can read in the Old Testament about the worship of beings like Moloch, who demanded sacrifices of little children burned alive. In other nations, the various evil spirits and fallen angels got men and women to worship them under other names. We know them as the Greek and Roman and Norse gods and goddesses and those in the myths of other cultures. In the Old Testament they are called the "Baalim," which refers to the evil "lords" or "gods" of the other nations (Judges 2:11, et al.).

When the devil was able to gain complete possession of a human being, he could use him or her to do a lot more damage, especially if he or she was in a position of power and authority, like the Emperor Nero, Caligula, or Ivan the Terrible, or in more modern days, Adolf Hitler, or Josef Stalin, both of whom were responsible for the murder of millions.

Involvement in the Psychic

Even if he cannot get people actively and knowingly to worship him, the enemy gets people involved in what is called "psychic phenomena." He tempts them to seek "spiritual experiences" by reaching out with their souls and bodies into the dark spiritual world around them. When people look to fortunetellers, clairvoyants, witches, sorcerers and suchlike to gain power and information from the spiritual realm, they open themselves for the enemy to gain more and more influence over them.[2]

All the way through the Scripture God warns against all such kinds of "occult" or psychic activities. Man is forbidden to try to reach out into the darkness around.

[2]For more information on the subject of the danger of the psychic read: Dennis and Rita Bennett, *The Holy Spirit and You* (Plainfield, N.J.: Logos 1971), pp. 36-55.

Summing Up

"Original sin" refers to man's condition of being separated from God. It leads to "actual sins," actual bad things people now began to do to one another—cheating, killing, lying, stealing, betrayals, hatefulness, selfishness. Through these actual bad deeds, man began to pile up guilt which further separated him from God, and gave Satan a further claim against him. The enemy could say to God, in effect, "Not only did these creatures rebel against you and turn their authority over to me, but now look at the sort of things they are doing to one another!"

So man is cut off from God in several ways. First, by the initial action of breaking fellowship with God and letting darkness take over the world, making it necessary for God to close off man's spirit. Next, man is separated from God by being under the domination of the "rulers of the darkness of this world," and often cooperating with them. Thirdly, he is separated by the wrong things he has actually done to his neighbors—his actual sins.

This whole disaster is referred to in theological terms as the "fall of man." It was a "fall" in two ways. First, because the human race fell away from God—was cut off from God, as we have seen. Secondly, we can look at it as a fall of man's spirit into bondage to man's soul.

The spirit is now unable to bring any inspiration or guidance to the soul. On the other hand, the spirit is entirely under the control of the soul.

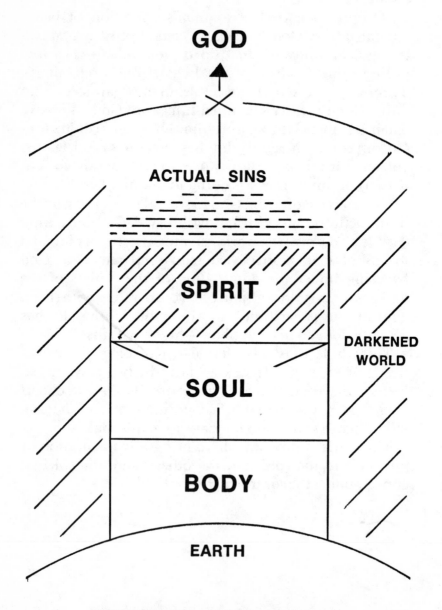

THREE-FOLD SEPARATION

10

Getting Back in Touch

God could have written man and his world off as a bad mistake, wiped it out, and begun over again somewhere else, but He didn't. If your children turned against you and took over your house, refusing to let you in, you wouldn't burn down the house with them in it, in an attempt to solve the problem, would you? Or to change the illustration, in a Western movie, the villain has grabbed the heroine and is using her for a shield. The hero won't shoot the villain, because if he did he'd shoot the heroine, which would plum spoil the story, to say nothing of spoiling the heroine! God loves the human creatures He has made, and won't give up on them. The Bible tells how He tried in many ways to penetrate the darkness and bridge the gap between Himself and mankind.

Man was spiritually cut off from God, but although Satan had usurped man's authority, he couldn't shut God out of the physical world. This is why the world of nature is such a contradiction. Haven't you ever wondered why nature could be at the same time so beautiful and so horrible? On the one hand, rivers and seas, trees and mountains, fascinating animals, birds, fishes, and other creatures; on the other hand, the cruelty and brutality of "Nature red in tooth and claw"—the violence and destructiveness of tornadoes, earthquakes, and floods.

So God could still appeal to man through his physical nature, his body, and once having gotten man's attention, God might then be able to influence his soul, and ultimately reach his spirit from that direction. That way, God could keep in touch with the human race and try to protect them from the enemy and his deceptions, until the basic problem could be solved and full relationship restored.

Very early on, Scripture tells how God succeeded with one man, Enoch. He "walked with God," and the Scripture says with simplicity, "He was not, for God took him!" (Gen. 5:24). He was sort of like a first fruits offering given to God out of the numbers of other people to come who would choose God rather than Satan.

It Began With Father Abraham

For the most part, though, it was a sad story. The world became so filled with violence that God, according to the book of Genesis, had to take the drastic measure of wiping them all away by a flood, leaving only the family of Noah (Gen. 6-9). But it wasn't long before man was in trouble again. The enemy's influence was just too strong. God Himself is quoted in Genesis 8:21 as saying: "The imagination of man's heart is evil from his youth. . . ."

God couldn't have fellowship with the people who were worshipping other gods, sacrificing their children, etc. He had to find someone who would listen to Him, and live the way He wanted.

Then God got the attention of a man called Abram, a wandering tribesman in Northern Arabia. He told Abraham (God renamed him): "If you will listen to Me and do what I say, I will bless you, and make you a blessing to other people. Your descendants," said God, "will bless every family in the whole world" (Gen. 12:1-3).

Abraham accepted God's offer, and God took care of him and his family, trying to teach them what He was like, and how He wanted them to live, so He could work through them to reach the rest of the world.

In order to do this He established a kind of "quarantine," and began separating Abraham's family from the rest of mankind. This was not because He was rejecting the rest of the world, but because He loved the whole human race and had a plan to rescue them from the enemy's clutches.

This special people had to have a place to live, so God provided for them what came to be called the Promised Land, a fertile strip of territory on the eastern end of the Mediterranean Sea, right at the heart of the ancient world.

Isaac Chosen

God began narrowing things down as people made their choices. Abraham had two sons; God picked Isaac to work through. Isaac had two, God chose Jacob as the successor. Jacob had twelve; they became the ancestors of the twelve tribes of Israel. Unfortunately, every time the Israelites became strong, some of them decided, just as Adam had, "We don't need God any more. We can handle things by ourselves. We'll call on God *if* we need Him!" Not only that, but they kept breaking the quarantine, and getting involved with the worship of evil spirits.

Judah Chosen

Through the centuries, ten of the tribes were eliminated, and of the remaining two, God selected one, the tribe of Judah, (from which we get the English word "Jew"). In all this process the "chosen" lost the Promised Land for a while, but they miraculously were brought back, at least a few of them, so that God's plan could be fulfilled.

How God's Spirit Moved Them

We said that in those days God was able to reach man's body, even though He could not contact him directly through the spirit. For some a temporary *physical* infilling of the Holy Spirit was all they were able to receive, but God was willing for this to happen, even though it sometimes resulted in men misusing the power.

Take Samson, for example, who under the influence of the "Spirit of the Lord" went down and killed thirty men, took their clothes, and paid off a bet! Not exactly an edifying story (Judges 14:19). Yet we need not doubt it was indeed the Spirit of God who gave Samson's body superhuman strength on this and other occasions. Samson's soul was undisciplined and headstrong, and so he could easily misuse the strength the Holy Spirit gave to his body. Some have described him as the "Lil Abner" of the Bible.

When the Spirit was able to penetrate further into human nature, He touched the soul. He was able to give Joseph the wisdom to become the number one man next to Pharaoh. It was Pharaoh himself who recognized that the Spirit of God was inspiring Joseph (Gen. 41:38).

Bezaleel, the man who made beautiful things for the Tabernacle, is an interesting case in point. Here God inspired both his soul and body, since Bezaleel had to have intelligence, aesthetic understanding, and also physical skill (Exod. 31:3).

With some, the Holy Spirit could touch the spirit. This gave people the ability to be "prophets."

A prophet in the Bible isn't someone, man or woman, who has power to foretell the future. The word in Hebrew means an "inspired person." The Greek word means a "forth-teller" (not a *fore*-teller). The prophets were people who were open enough to God that He could communicate to them messages He wanted them to pass along to others. "This is what the Lord is saying."

True, this often resulted in a fore-telling of things to come, but in the Bible this is typically: "*If* you don't do this or that, such and such will happen." The future to the prophet is simply what God is going to do, not a fixed and predetermined fate.

God's Plan

In all this God had an incredible plan. He was going to come to earth so that people could *see* and *experience* what He was like. Since He couldn't come to them through the spiritual door, He would come to them physically, as part of the material world. He couldn't come in His power and glory; the evil world could not have survived that. His plan was to come as a man among men. He would actually live among human beings as one of them.

God had said to Abraham, "I'm going to bless you, and make you a blessing, and through your seed all families of the earth are going to be blessed" (Gen. 12:3).

All this selecting and narrowing down God had been going through was to come to a point in one Person. He was going to be the "Seed" through whom all the families of the earth could be blessed.

Mary Chosen

The narrowing process focused on a Judaean young woman, engaged but not yet married, Mary of Nazareth. God sent the angel Gabriel to announce to her that she was to be the mother of a most special child. (Even at this critical point God respected human free will. Mary could have said, "no," and it might have taken God many more years to carry out His plan.) Mary consented, even though it meant risking her reputation, and perhaps even her life. The Israelites still officially had the death penalty for a woman bearing a child ostensibly out of wedlock. God's Spirit touched Mary's body, and Jesus was conceived.

Mary's child was going to be both fully God and fully human. He was going to be the Rescuer, who could solve man's threefold problem. God had spoken to man through the darkness. Some had listened, but the real solution began when God penetrated the darkness to bring about the Incarnation.

The Plan Carried Out

"In the fulness of time"—that is, just at the right point when everything was ready—Jesus was conceived and born (Heb. 10:5). God didn't just put on a human body as a kind of disguise or costume, He really became human—joined Himself permanently to human flesh.

This is why the teaching about the Virgin Birth is so important. The Spirit of God actually fertilized a human ovum so that the fetus was literally and physically both God and man.

How could God become a human? This question baffled the Hebrew people in whose midst He was born and grew up, since they didn't understand what later some came to realize, that God is a "divine community" in Himself: three persons, totally distinct from one another, and yet perfectly united in one godhead. It was the second person of the Trinity who came to earth and became a man. We call Him God, the Son. Although His relationship to the Father is more wonderful than any human father-son relationship could be, it isn't *less* than that, and we can understand it best in those terms.

Jesus was born and grew up physically and psychologically like other human beings. "And Jesus increased in wisdom [soul-*psuche*] and stature [body] and in favor with God and man" (Luke 2:52, KJV). ". . . The child grew, and became strong in spirit [*pneuma* in Greek], filled with wisdom . . ." (Luke 2:40, KJV modernized). So Jesus had a spirit, soul and body as we do. But His Spirit was always in fellowship with God.

What was Jesus like when He was little? Did He go around working miracles, as some of the old legends say? Or was He a normal boy? As a child working in His dad's shop, if something wasn't quite square after it was finished, did Jesus miraculously adjust it, as another story says? No. As far as we can tell, Jesus did not do any "mighty works" until He was thirty years old. When He returned to His home town after He had begun His ministry, they didn't say, "Oh, here's Jesus come back home. We're so proud of Him. He's been doing those miracles out there that He used to do at home." No, they said, "Well, here's the carpenter's son finally come back! Who does He think He is, anyway? Let's see Him do some of the things He's supposedly been doing down there in

Capernaum!" They didn't believe in Him, and at that time He could do very little in Nazareth.

Jesus was thirty when He began the work He'd come to do, but first He was baptized in the Holy Spirit. The Holy Spirit had always been in Him, from the very beginning of His life on earth, but the Spirit needed to be released with power, then the power could begin to pour out (Luke 3:22, 4:1, et al.). He went around doing the sort of things His Father would have done. He "went about doing good" (Acts 10:38). He healed sickness at every opportunity. He cast out evil spirits. He did everything possible to correct the mess that had been made of the world after it fell into Satan's hands.

The Enemy Retaliates

Satan, of course, struck back as soon as he was able. He stirred up some of the political and religious leaders against Jesus, and they finally succeeded in getting Him killed as a dangerous rabble-rouser. Jesus, of course, didn't have to let this happen, but He knew His death was necessary to rescue the human race, so He allowed Himself to be arrested, tried, and crucified (Matt. 26:53, John 18:6, et al.).

When Jesus died, He made a complete settlement for all the bad things done by humans, from the beginning to the end of history. The Scripture says that although Jesus was without sin, He was "made sin" for us. Like the scapegoat in the Old Testament, Jesus bore our sins on the cross, and thus experienced the separation caused by sin.[1] Just before He died, He cried out, "My God, My God, why hast thou

[1] We often miss the fact that there were *two* scapegoats in the Bible. One of them was the creature upon whom the sins of the people were symbolically laid, and this goat was driven out into the wilderness. The other goat was sacrificed as a whole burnt offering. Jesus fulfilled both types. As the sin-bearing goat He was driven into the wilderness and experienced the agony of separation from God for a while. As the "Lord's Goat," Jesus continued to offer Himself perfectly to His Father, even though it meant that the

forsaken me?" For a time He experienced what hell *is,* separation from God.

Then as the fellowship was restored, Jesus said, "Father, I put my Spirit in your hands" (Mark 15:34, Luke 23:46) and allowed Himself to die. He "performed a death," or "accomplished an exodus" as it says in Luke 9:31.

After He died, He invaded the darkness to the very bottom, and went to the souls who were being held prisoner by Satan (1 Pet. 3:19). Those who accepted Him, He set free and they accompanied Him back to the Father's House. He "led captivity captive," as Paul said to the Ephesians (Eph. 4:8).

Jesus Paid Our Debt

All this was part of the plan. In Jesus, God completely identified Himself with us—spirit, soul and body. When Jesus let Himself be killed by the dark powers infesting the world, He canceled every claim Satan had against the human race because of the terrible things they had done, and would yet do.

Imagine a young man who comes to his dad and says, "Dad, I've just got to talk to you! I've embezzled money from the firm I work for. It now comes to over $100,000 and I've spent it all. What shall I do?"

His father could say, "Well, uh, that's okay, son. Don't worry about it. After all, you *are* my son, and I love you. It's okay. Forget it!"

The son would be even more distressed. "But, dad! I told you about my taking the money because I knew it was wrong, and I felt guilty. But now you're just as bad as I am!"

But since the father in our story is an honest man, he

hatred of men in the darkened world would bring Him to a painful and shameful death. The word "sacrifice" doesn't necessarily mean suffering. It means being totally obedient, making a perfect offering. It is only in an evil world that sacrifice involves suffering.

says instead, "Son, you've got to go to the authorities and confess what you've done, and take your punishment, even if it means going to jail." That's justice. But then the father says, "But I'll tell you what. I love you so much I'm going to mortgage our home and sell the car, cash in my insurance—do everything in my power to pay off your debt. If they'd let me, I'd serve your jail sentence for you!"

God is a God of fairness, and He could not say to human beings, even when we are sorry for our sins, "It doesn't matter; I love you, just forget the whole thing!"

The responsibility has to be met. Our sins have to be paid for, or else God would not be just. But with the death of Jesus, God Himself took care of them, and for any person who accepts Jesus, the pile of sins separating him from God is cleared away.

By bringing about the death of Jesus, Satan defeated himself. By dying on the cross Jesus canceled the guilt of mankind from the beginning to the end of human history, for those who would receive Him.

Jesus served our prison sentence for us; He became the hostage in the heroine's place; He went into the captured house to reconcile God with His rebellious children.

11

The Hope

Can you imagine going to over to visit your friends, and having the lady of the house say proudly, "I want to show you my clean dishes!" Whereupon she opens the kitchen cupboards and displays all her carefully washed china for your admiration! It isn't too likely someone would do this, although when you sit down to dinner you are glad, if you happen to think about it, to know the hostess *did* wash the dishes! However, she didn't wash them to display them, but to use them. To fill them!

Jesus died so we could be forgiven, but if we stop with that, and go no further, it's like washing the dishes but never sitting down to eat and drink from the nicely cleaned plates and cups. If you never intended to reuse the dishes, you wouldn't even bother to keep them around, unless they were some kind of family heirloom—then they *might* just sit on the shelf and be proudly displayed! (Could there be some *people* like that?) Jesus didn't just come to wash us and show us off: "Look at all the forgiven sinners I've got!"

Forgiveness Is Not Enough

In Scandinavia Dennis was asked to speak at a luncheon, and was seated next to one of the high church officials of the area. Following Dennis's talk about the power of the Spirit, this man said earnestly, "You know, Dennis, my experience of the Holy Spirit is that I daily feel the warmth of sin forgiven. That's enough for me."

To this, Dennis could only answer, "Yes, I agree, that is the first great work of the Spirit. But there's more!"

When the Atonement of Jesus is spoken of it's usually referring to His death on the cross. The word is used in the sense of "make up for," or "pay for." But that isn't what "atone" means.[1] "Atone" is literally made up of the two words "at one." Atonement is "at-one-ment." It was Jesus' death on the cross that made the "at-one-ment" *possible*, but the actual "at-one-ment" happens *after* we've been forgiven, when we are reunited with God.

We'll say you've quarreled with a friend and then made up. You go to visit him, but when he opens the door and invites you in, you just stand in the doorway, smiling and happy. Your friend has forgiven you, but until you have actually gone inside, your "at-one-ment" with your friend is not complete.

Jesus dying on the cross canceled the claims Satan had against us for the actual wrong things we had done to one another, but if that were the whole story, we would still be separated from God (1 Cor. 15:14, 17). We would be without hope of life; our faith would be pointless. But Jesus didn't stay dead, and when He rose from the dead He opened the way for us to come back into direct personal relationship with God. This cancellation of our sin and separation makes a new kind of relationship with God possible. Paul calls it: "Christ in you, the hope of glory" (Col. 1:27).

---

[1] The word is only used once in the Authorized Version of the New Testament, and that is to translate Greek *katallage*, which means "restoration to fellowship," "reconciliation."

Before Jesus' time, in Old Testament days as we've seen, the Holy Spirit could temporarily fill people from body to soul to spirit; there were Elijah, Elisha, the seventy elders under Moses, King Saul, and others. John the Baptist, still an "Old Testament" person, was "filled with the Holy Spirit from his mother's womb" (Luke 1:15). Elizabeth, John's mother, was "filled with the Holy Spirit" at the same time, when her cousin Mary, newly impregnated with the life of Jesus, came into her presence.

Yet Jesus said the "least in the kingdom" was greater than John the Baptist because these earlier infillings of God's Spirit were only temporary. But beginning with Jesus Himself a new kind of relationship between human beings and God became possible. Jesus was born of the Holy Spirit, and being the eternal Son of God, the second person of the blessed Trinity, He and the Holy Spirit had always been joined in perfect fellowship. Jesus was the first human being with the Holy Spirit permanently living in Him.

During His time on earth before His resurrection, Jesus could give the Holy Spirit to others temporarily, in the Old Testament way. He gave His disciples temporary power to heal the sick and throw out demons (Luke 10:1-20, et al.). He gave Peter power to walk on water, temporarily (Matt. 14:30). John 7:39 says that "The Holy Ghost was not yet given, [permanently] because that Jesus was not yet glorified."

After He rose from the dead and had His glorified body, He was able to give the Holy Spirit in a new way, permanently: "I will ask the Father, and He will give you another helper just like me, who will remain with you *forever*: the Spirit of truth, whom the world cannot receive because it doesn't see Him or know Him, but you know

Him, for He's staying with you now, and will be *in* you" (John 14:16, 17, author's literal translation). "The water [Holy Spirit] that I shall give," says Jesus, "shall be *in* you a well of water springing up into everlasting life" (John 4:14b).

A New Relationship With God

On the evening of the day He rose from death, Jesus went to His friends where they were having supper together in an upstairs apartment. They'd had some reports of Jesus' resurrection, which they didn't quite believe. Jesus came in through the locked doors, and after reassuring them He was not a ghost, ate supper with them (John 20:19).

The barrier of sin had been cleared away by His death, and Satan was defeated by His resurrection, so now there was nothing to prevent Jesus from giving the Holy Spirit to His friends in this new and permanent way. God had closed the door of the human spirit so it could not be opened to the fallen spiritual world of Satan that surrounded it, the psychic world, but now that Jesus has come, and defeated Satan on his own ground, God can allow people to open the door of their spirits to Jesus. Jesus said He was the door (John 10:9). He is the door to God's spiritual kingdom, and when we open our doors to Him, the darkness cannot come in, but the Holy Spirit can. "Behold," says Jesus, "I stand at the door and knock" (Rev. 3:20).

The human *will* is still in the picture. *We* have to open the door. Jesus, the Scripture says (John 20), "breathed on them" and then directed *them* to admit the Holy Spirit. Here are two separate actions. When Jesus breathed on them, He was offering them new life in the Spirit, but they

76

still had to *receive* the Gift. He did not breathe the Spirit *into* them, He breathed *upon* them. It was up to them to allow the Holy Spirit to come *in*. The sun can be shining outside but you have to open the shades before it can shine into your home.

The disciples did choose to receive the new life and so became the first "born-again" people. Their human spirits now became holy places, special sanctuaries in the center of their beings where the Holy Spirit could take up permanent residence. The first human beings had been in fellowship with God externally, and they had broken the relationship. The relationship with God is no longer outside, but inside, so it can't be broken by transitory feelings or careless actions.

Paul says of this new relationship, "If any man be in Christ, he is a *new creation*," he or she is recreated, regenerated, "born again." A new kind of human being has come into existence, patterned after Jesus. Jesus is God living in a human body, and that's what the new kind of human being is too. Fellowship with God has been renewed, but it is no longer external, it is now happening right inside the person, because the Holy Spirit is inside.

Rita likes to use this illustration to describe what Jesus does for the human spirit. She says, "Hold out your hands. Now make your left hand into a fist—that represents your fallen spirit which became atrophied and dead to God. Let your right hand represent the Holy Spirit. When you received Jesus, the Holy Spirit breathed resurrection life into your dead spirit and it came alive. Now hold your open right hand over your left fist, thus symbolizing God's Spirit overshadowing your spirit. Open your left fist, showing your spirit receiving resurrection life from the Holy Spirit.

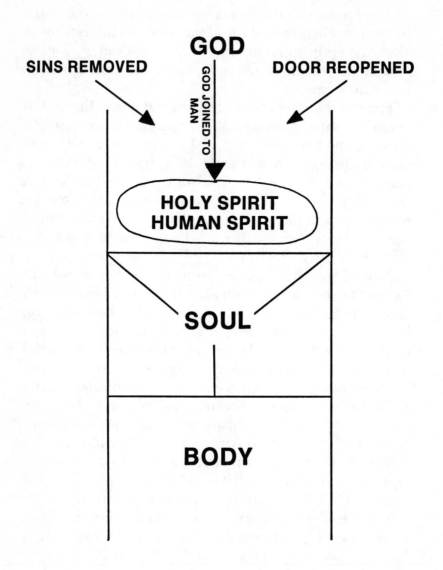

THE NEW CREATURE

"Now look at your hands again. They are distinct from one another. Although God lives in you, He's an individual being, and you are an individual being. It's not true, as some teach, that when you become a Christian you are swallowed up in God and no longer continue to exist. God delights in you as an individual person. For all of this you can lift both your hands and praise the Lord!

"Now lace your fingers together. You and God have been joined together permanently in a love relationship. You and God are one in Spirit. 'He that is joined unto the Lord is one spirit' (1 Cor. 6:17). Although you are still an individual person, yet you are united with Him."

And this relationship is secure. Wouldn't it have been terrible if Jesus had merely canceled our sins, bringing us back to the same state of innocence Adam and Eve had before they fell? If our continuing relationship with God still depended on *us* holding on to Him, how long do you think it would have taken us to break it again?

God's Image in You

There's much more to it! The first human pair were God's beloved human creatures, special because they were made in God's image. They had the ability to respond to God, and to enjoy His friendship.

After God's Spirit comes to live in us, however, we now become sons and daughters of God, part of the family. We can say and experience "Our Father." We are co-heirs with Jesus, who is our elder brother. As the father said to the older son in the story of the Prodigal, "All I have is yours" (Luke 15:31b), so God says this to all His sons and daughters.

When we say we're made in the image of God, we really are talking about two things. First, we're saying that our spirits are made like God who is Spirit, so we can respond to Him.

The second, and much broader meaning of being made in God's image, is to be made like Him in *character*. A man may have a son who resembles him in physical features, but is not a bit like his father in personality. The father is outgoing, the son is reserved; the father is even-tempered, the son is quick-tempered. A friend who knew them both might comment, "Jack is just the image of his father, yet he's not very much like him in temperament."

If we could go back to the Garden of Eden and meet Adam or Eve in their newly created glory, we would meet two Christ-like people, for God created them in His image in both senses of the word. They were not only made like Him in having spiritual natures, but they were like Him in character—God expressed in human terms. When they turned from God, and broke the relationship, the first kind of image remained; they still had spirits, though spirits dead to God. There was still the possibility that some day the fellowship might be renewed. The "apparatus" was still there, so to speak, but it was put out of action. In the second sense of the word, the image and likeness of God very rapidly decayed.

Jesus does two things for us when we are born again of the Spirit. First, He brings our spirits alive to God, so that once more we can respond to Him, and second, the character of God begins to be reestablished in us. As Paul puts it, we "put on the new man, which is renewed in knowledge after the image of him that created him" (Col. 3:10). The Greek word for "image" here means pattern and moral and spiritual likeness.

His likeness in you means His character or nature will now be able to be seen in you. If you respond out of the reservoir of His life in you, there will be love when you need it, and joy and peace too. You'll be able to forgive even when your soul doesn't want to. When your physical and psychological drives need to be disciplined, God's resources are there to be drawn upon. The character of God is actually the "fruit of the Spirit" (Gal. 5:22, 23).

What else is so great about having a recreated spirit? Without it God couldn't live in you. Every time you sin the Holy Spirit would have to leave because He won't dwell in sin. You'd have to get born of the Spirit over and over again. Fortunately our spirits don't sin since we've been born of God's incorruptible life; even when our *souls* sin God remains in that holy place within (1 John 3:8, 9; 1 Peter 1:23, 3:4; 2 Peter 1:4; Heb. 12:23b; Ps. 32:2).

What else is it? It's the secret dwelling place of God, a place of rest, a place of receiving God's wisdom and truth, a place where communication with God is possible, a place of direction and guidance, a place of ageless or eternal life, a place of quickening for you and from where you can speak life to others, a place of strength. Need we say more? (Ps. 91:1; Eph. 2:6; 1 Peter 2:4; Ps. 51:6b; Rom. 8:27; 1 Cor. 2:11-15; John 4:23, 24; Ps. 42:7a; Rom. 8:16; Prov. 20:27; Ps. 18:28; John 3:16; 1 Cor. 15:45; Eph. 3:16)

Paul talks of the mystery which has been hidden through the ages, but is now revealed to us, "Christ in you, the hope of glory" (Col. 1:27). Without Jesus' life in us there would be no hope for our lives or for anyone else, but with Him there is hope for us, hope for the world, hope for the future. Christ in me, Christ in you—the hope.

If you're not sure you've received this new life, by opening your heart and life to Jesus, make sure right now by speaking these words. Here is an outline to follow:

> Dear Father in heaven, I'm lost and without purpose. I've done a lot of wrong things that hurt myself and others, and I want to be different, but I can't do it alone. Because of Jesus' death and resurrection for me, I can ask You to forgive all my wrong behavior and rebellion (sins). I accept Your forgiveness, Father, and, Jesus, I ask You to come into my spirit. Bring me alive to You and the Father by the power of Your Holy Spirit. Give me new life, new direction and hope. Thank You, Jesus, for coming into my life. I know You're living in me right now. I renounce you, Satan, and any hold you might have had on me. I cast you out, and all other wrong spirits, bound and tied, in the name of Jesus, and under His precious blood.
>
> Thank You, Father, for restoring me to the character and likeness of Jesus. I forgive everyone who ever hurt me. I also forgive myself. Thank You, Father, Jesus, and Holy Spirit. In Jesus' name!

It's a good idea to make a permanent record for your own reminder, sign it and date it.

12

Channels for Power

That ought to solve all the problems! People with God actually living in them, just like Jesus. And sure enough these first friends of Jesus went all over the place doing the sort of things He'd been doing. They healed the sick, set people free from evil spirits, even raised the dead. The complaint about them was they "turned the world upside down" (Acts 17:6). The world was already standing on its head, and the Christians turned it the right way up, but of course the world didn't see it that way!

But wait a minute! Those first people did not *immediately* go out and turn the world upside down. As a matter of fact, Jesus Himself told them not to try it. His last instructions to them were "sit down and wait" (Luke 24:49, literal Greek). Why? Because there were still two things that had to happen before Jesus' people could begin their work in the world. The first was that the Spirit of God had to be poured out "upon all flesh."

After all, those first friends of Jesus had come into direct contact with Him, so that He could give them the Holy

Spirit, but how is He going to reach the rest of mankind? How are *we* going to get the blessings? Did you ever stop to think what it would have been like if Jesus had remained on the earth after His resurrection, and we still had to come into direct contact with Him in order to be reborn of the Spirit, healed, or even get a prayer through to the Father? Can you imagine the billions of people waiting in line to see Jesus? You'd have to wait twenty years just to get near Him. It would be a tragically impossible situation.

How Jesus Solved the Problem

We take it for granted that we can contact God at any time, and forget that it wasn't always so. Something had to happen before it would be possible for human beings everywhere to receive the wonderful ministry of Jesus.

One day, during His time on earth before His resurrection, He was talking to the people and they were crowding to get close to Him. Jesus climbed into Peter's boat and asked him to push off a little way from the shore. Then Jesus could talk to the people more effectively. All of them could see Him and hear Him.

So there came a day when Jesus "pushed off" from the earth. He ascended into heaven so He could reach everybody who wanted Him. He took some of His disciples and went up on the Mount of Olives, and there, as they watched, He was "taken up, and a cloud received Him out of their sight" (Acts 1:9). They went home and waited as He had told them to, and after ten days, on the Hebrew feast of Pentecost, the Holy Spirit was "poured out on all flesh." God had come to them in a new way. While Jesus was still on the earth after His resurrection, in His glorified body, He could give new life in the Spirit permanently to those who came in direct contact with Him, and would receive it.

When Jesus ascended back to the Father, physical contact with Him was broken for a while, but the Holy Spirit was still living in those first people.

Poured Out on the World

Jesus took His place at the right hand of God and then on the Day of Pentecost the Spirit was poured out on the whole world.

After this it was possible for any human being, anywhere in the world, to receive new life in the Spirit. When you tell someone about Jesus, you don't have to take Jesus to them. He is already there. All they have to do is open the door and ask Him to come in! By His ascending into heaven, and by the coming of the Holy Spirit, it is now possible for Jesus to reach anyone, anywhere.

13

Release in Soul and Body

Jesus had told His followers to "sit down and wait" before they went out to tell the world about Him, because the Holy Spirit had to be poured out from heaven "upon all flesh" before Jesus would be available to everyone.

But there was a second reason. The Holy Spirit not only had to be made available to the whole world, He had to be released with power in the lives of those who had received Jesus. Just as the Holy Spirit was always living in Jesus, but had to be released with power before Jesus could begin His ministry, so with the people who are born again of the Spirit, the Spirit's power needed to be released in *them* before they went out to spread the Word. Jesus' last instruction before He went back to His Father was to receive this "baptism in the Holy Spirit" as He called it. They were not to leave Jerusalem, He said, until they had been "endued with power." Notice that He wasn't talking about salvation. He didn't say to His friends, "Wait until you are born again" or "Wait here until your sins are forgiven," or even "Wait here until you are *given* the Holy

Spirit." After all, He had made the Holy Spirit available to them forty days before (John 20), and now He is telling them to wait for another experience in which the Holy Spirit will "come upon them" in power.

Did you ever say something like "I don't know what came over me. I was suddenly overwhelmed with love for him (or her)." Where did this love come from that "came upon you"? From inside you. Something inside you was responding to a stimulus outside you. So with this enduement with power by the Holy Spirit. The Holy Spirit was living in these men and women because they had received Him directly from Jesus. Now the Spirit living in them was going to overwhelm them with His presence, as He was poured out on the whole world.

Most of you reading this have an automobile somewhere nearby; in the driveway or in the garage. It may be the latest model, or not quite so new. It may be a Rolls-Royce, or a VW Beetle, but one thing's for sure, it has a *battery*! (That is, of course, unless you own an early Model T Ford and are still hand-cranking!) The battery contains electricity. It's highly important that it does have a hundred or so ampere-hours of juice in it, when you go to start your car. But it won't do any good at all to have the electricity in the battery unless it *flows out*. Did your car ever fail to start, and you checked the battery only to find it fully charged? Then you discovered the cables were not properly connected so that the power could flow from the battery to the starter motor? God is living in the re-created human spirit. It's clear enough, though, that He's got to be able to flow *out* into the soul and body, before He can reach the world.

When the Holy Spirit was poured out "upon all flesh" at Pentecost, the disciples (120 of them) in whom He was already living, began to respond. They began to overflow. The Spirit was not just stirred within them, He began to pour out of their spirits, into their souls, into their bodies, and out into the world. They began to celebrate and rejoice, probably to laugh and cry and sing and dance with joy! But the glory of God flowed mainly out of their most important channels and organs of expression, their voices.

Dogs and cats and birds could have danced and jumped and barked and sung as the joy of the Lord touched them, but only humans among the creatures of earth could have opened their mouths in meaningful words of praise and thanks, as they did. Not only did they do this in their own language, but in languages they had never learned or heard, so strong was the inspiration of the Holy Spirit in them. This drew a great deal of attention, especially since spiritual power began to show through them in other ways.

Peter and John healed a crippled man (Acts 3) and soon there was such a flood of healing that people were struggling to touch even Peter's shadow (Acts 5:15).

The Holy Spirit had come to live in their spirits, and they had become "new creatures." Now when the Holy Spirit was poured out on the whole world, because He was already living in them they responded, and the new life began to pour out of their spirits into their souls and into their bodies, and so out into the world around. This is the "baptism in the Holy Spirit." It means that now their whole beings were inundated with the Holy Spirit, and the power of God was flowing out through their hands and feet and voices.

So you can see when the Holy Spirit is released from where He is living in the human spirit, the first thing that

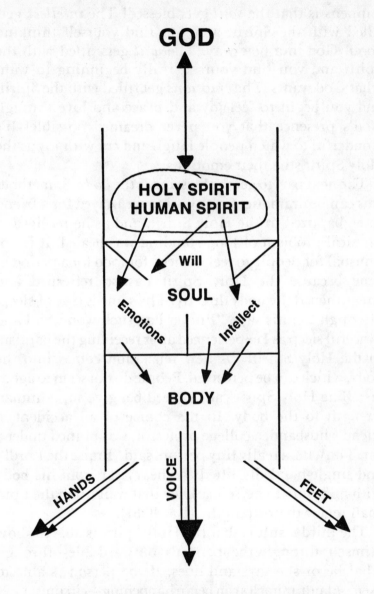

GOD

HOLY SPIRIT
HUMAN SPIRIT

Will

SOUL

Emotions   Intellect

BODY

HANDS   VOICE   FEET

THE RELEASE OF THE SPIRIT

happens is that the *soul* gets blessed! The *intellect* gets filled with the Spirit, and you find yourself thinking about God in a new way. The *will* gets filled with the Spirit and you find yourself really beginning to want what God wants. The *emotions* get filled with the Spirit, and you begin to feel joy and peace and love through God's presence that you never dreamed possible! It's wonderful to watch people laugh and cry with joy as the Holy Spirit stirs their emotions.

The next part to get the blessing is the *body*. Sometimes this can be dramatic. One evening we prayed for a friend to be baptized in the Holy Spirit, and as he received, a physical problem of long standing was healed. It is not unusual for people to feel no need for food for a period of time because the Holy Spirit has so refreshed and strengthened the body directly. The same is true of sleep, although Dennis says, "I never had such wonderful and peaceful sleep as I experienced after receiving the baptism in the Holy Spirit!" A new relaxation comes into the body, which can be perceived. People do not seem to age as fast. The Holy Spirit can, if need be, give superhuman strength to the body. In the course of an accident, a friend's husband, a college professor, was pinned under a car. The wife, a really tiny person, said "Praise the Lord!" and single-handedly lifted the heavy car from his body with no injury to herself. "They that wait upon the Lord shall renew their strength" (Isa. 40:31).

The third result is that the Holy Spirit is able to show Himself through the person's outward life—through what he or she says and does. If the person is able to exercise faith, miracles can begin happening—circumstances will change to be more as God wants them to be.

One Baptism in Two Parts

Some are troubled at the phrase "baptism in the Holy Spirit." We could set it aside and not use it, but Jesus used it, and so did Peter and John the Baptist and many others in the New Testament, so we can't very well ignore it. The expression is confusing in the first place because we think of baptism as a ceremony in which a person is sprinkled with, washed with, or dipped into water. The word "baptize," however, is really the intensive form of the Greek verb *bapto* which means to dip. *Baptizo* in classical Greek means to sink, drench, be waterlogged, to be totally and permanently overwhelmed by, or in, another element such as water. It is used in classical Greek to describe a sunken, waterlogged ship. (This, by the way, is why all arguments about modes of baptism are so futile. No ceremony of baptism, whether sprinkling, pouring, or immersing, can fully symbolize what the word "baptize" means. You just can't leave people under the water in the baptistry, or in the river, yet if you are "baptized into Christ" you don't want to be taken out again, do you?)

The baptism in the Holy Spirit means, then, that the Holy Spirit, who is living in the human spirit because of Jesus, now flows out to inundate soul and body, and flows out to the world around.

"But I thought the Bible said there is only one baptism?" It does, and it also says there are more than one! Jesus Himself said, "John truly baptized with water; but ye shall be baptized with the Holy Ghost . . ." (Acts 1:5). The book of Hebrews speaks of the doctrine of *baptisms* (Heb. 6:2). Why?

There *is* just one baptism, but this one baptism has two aspects that can sometimes be quite distinct. There is an *in*flow, when the Holy Spirit comes to dwell in you and baptizes your spirit, this is salvation, the new birth; and there is an *out*flow, when the Spirit living in you is released from your spirit to baptize or inundate your soul and body, and so out into the world around.

When Jesus spoke of being "baptized in the Holy Spirit" it seems clear He was speaking of this *outflow*. In John 7:37-39 He says, "If any man thirst, let him come unto me and drink"—this is referring to the coming in of the Spirit. Then He continued, "If a man believe in me, out of his belly shall flow rivers of living water." Here Jesus is clearly talking of the second part of one process. The living water flows in, and then flows out.

He did the same with the woman at the well in Samaria. He said, "I would give you living water, and you'd never thirst again." But then He added, "The water that I give you will be in you a well of water springing up unto everlasting life!" (John 4:14).

Some will say they were "baptized in the Holy Spirit" when they first received Jesus. We understand this if they mean that their *spirits* were baptized. The process then needs to be completed by allowing the Holy Spirit to baptize or inundate the soul and body. All Christians have allowed Him to flow *in*, but most still seriously limit His *out*flow.

After a person receives the baptism in the Holy Spirit, Jesus' work in him is able to be completed. The life of God is coming in through the spirit, inspiring the soul, the soul is directing the body, and so the life of God is flowing right through into the world around. Now there is hope for humans, and for human society. The kingdom of God can begin to come on the earth.

14

Setting Your Spirit Free

How is this freedom or release of the Spirit—what Jesus calls the baptism in the Holy Spirit—to be received? We accept Jesus very simply—is there also a simple way to release the Holy Spirit?

Our present study gives us a clue, for if the baptism in the Holy Spirit is an outflow of the Spirit from where He dwells in the spirit to flood the soul and body and overflow into the world, then it's clear that receiving the baptism in the Holy Spirit is not something God does, but something the person receiving does. It is a response, an opening of soul and body to the work of the Holy Spirit.

This is why the word "receive" is used rather than "get" or "acquire." God has already given the Holy Spirit to live in the person, but now he or she needs to *receive* the gift, by allowing Him free access to the soul and body.

How Do We Make Him Welcome in the Soul?

Some would say the first step is to get the emotions stirred up. This might be called the "old time" approach!

You get people as excited as possible, and perhaps something will happen! This doesn't work very well.

Emotion is good. Who would want to live without emotion? When God touches the emotions, they will respond as He wants them to, but the baptism in the Holy Spirit doesn't come from the emotions, but from the spirit. If the emotions are just stirred up and excited they can get in the way of the Holy Spirit's flow instead of helping.

The part played by the emotions is to respond to the joy, peace, and love of the Holy Spirit, and this is wonderful; but it is a response, not the source.

Others approach the question intellectually. "I will *believe* I have received the baptism with the Holy Spirit," they say. This is usually referred to as "receiving by faith" but it's actually an effort to believe with the intellect.

It doesn't work either. It's as if Peter had said, "I believe I can walk on the water! I receive 'walking on the water' by faith," without ever budging from the boat! Would that have been faith?

The Holy Spirit isn't asking us to *try* to believe something, or to understand something. At this point we aren't concerned with the intellect. The only thing needed to be done for the intellect in preparing a person to receive the baptism in the Holy Spirit is to answer as many of his sincere questions as possible. We find that the more we can reassure the intellect, the better, so that it can step aside, and let the Spirit work.

The intellect, like the emotions, can appreciate and enjoy what the Holy Spirit is doing—emotions and intellect are both to be filled to overflowing with His blessing.

But the *will* is involved directly in the process. The

Holy Spirit does ask that we be *willing* to receive Him into our souls and bodies. The will is the doorkeeper of the soul that opens the soul to the Holy Spirit. God won't break down the door. "I must choose to receive the power and freedom of the Spirit. I am willing for God to fill me to overflowing with His life!"

The Body's Response

What next then? The next response is from the *body*. We are inviting the Holy Spirit to flow through from our spirits to our souls to our bodies, and so out to the world around. There must be cooperation all the way.

The will is ready to allow the Spirit to flow into the soul, but how can the body respond? When we read the Acts of the Apostles we get a clue. There seems to be a common factor in the examples of people who were baptized in the Holy Spirit. In all but one case in the Acts of the Apostles, when the Holy Spirit was received with power, people began to *speak*, not just in their own languages, but in new languages they did not know with their intellects, which were given directly by the Holy Spirit. The speaking *out* seems to be the common factor.

In Acts 2, 10, 11, and 19 this phenomenon is explicit, whereas in Acts 8 it is implied; yet leading commentators agree that the key manifestation here also was speaking in tongues. Matthew Henry, for example, comments on Acts 8:14ff.: "It is said (v. 16) 'The Holy Ghost was as yet fallen upon none of them,' in those extraordinary powers which were conveyed by the descent of the Spirit upon the Day of Pentecost. They were none of them endued with the gift of tongues,[1] which seems then to have been the most usual immediate effect on the pouring out of the Spirit.... They laid their hands on them . . . upon the use of this sign,

[1] Note that Matthew Henry does not distinguish between the "gift of tongues," which is for the edifying of the Church, and must be accompanied by the gift of interpretation, and speaking in tongues as a private prayer language.

'they received the Holy Ghost, and spoke with tongues.' "[2]

Lalein Glossais

Paul calls it *lalein glossais*, which in Greek means: "speaking in languages," but which King James translators rendered "speaking in tongues." The word "tongue" is most commonly used by us today to refer to the physical member of the body, but in Elizabethan times it was commonly used as a synonym for "spoken language." (We, of course, still use it that way, but it has become a bit archaic to say, "He spoke in the French tongue," for example.) It seems to have been normative for the early Christians to pray and praise and prophesy in a special way, directly by the inspiration of the Holy Spirit. It was this "speaking in tongues" that attracted so much attention and led directly to three thousand people being converted on the day of Pentecost.

This was a brand new thing God had reserved for His New Covenant people. It had never occurred before Pentecost. Certainly one of its values *was* the attention it attracted. It caused people to ask, "What does it mean?" (Acts 2:12) which gave believers, like Peter in Acts 2, a chance to tell about Jesus. It was taken as a clear sign that the Holy Spirit was in action.

Explanation of Speaking by the Spirit

How does this make sense? Why should such a seemingly incidental and irrational activity have so much to do with the freedom of the Holy Spirit? The answer lies in understanding what "speaking in tongues" is—and where it comes from.

What is our chief means of expression? The other day Dennis was at his desk. The telephone rang. It was a friend

---

[2]Matthew Henry, *A Commentary on the Whole Bible*, (Revell) Vol. VI, page 100.

calling from Kyoto, Japan. As he talked, Dennis's voice took him to Japan with virtually no effort. How much effort would it have taken for his arms or legs to take him there?

If you are the owner or manager of a business, which would hamper you most, to have a sprained ankle that kept you from the office for a couple of weeks, or to have a case of laryngitis so you were not allowed to use your voice for two weeks? Think about it. You know that even though you couldn't walk, you could get on the phone and direct things at the office pretty well, but what is more frustrating than to sit at a desk unable to talk to people and have to write everything down, or make gestures?

The Scripture in many places emphasizes the importance of the voice: "A man's belly shall be satisfied with the fruit of his *mouth*; and with the increase of his *lips* shall he be filled. Death and life are in the power of the *tongue*: and they that love it shall eat the fruit thereof" (Prov. 18:20, 21). "Out of the *mouth* of babes and sucklings hast thou ordained strength . . ." (Ps. 8:2). "By the *word* of the Lord were the heavens made; and all the host of them by the breath of his *mouth*" (Ps. 33:6). "He *spoke* and it was done" (Ps. 33:9). ". . . whosoever shall *say* to this mountain, Be thou removed, and be thou cast into the sea; and shall not doubt in his heart, but shall believe that those things which he *saith* shall come to pass; he shall have whatsoever he *saith*" (italics ours throughout) (Mark 11:23).

The third chapter of James compares the tongue to the bit in a horse's mouth by which the animal is guided. If you can control the voice you can control the whole person. Psychologists understand very well the power of the tongue. Something that is put into words has far greater influence than something that is still just a thought in the mind. We drew the voice arrow larger than the others because it represents the main gate through which a person expresses himself. The Holy Spirit wants to inspire your spirit, and then flood your soul—will, thoughts, feelings, and so on, into your body and out to the world.

The voice is the main gate by which the Holy Spirit is going to reach the world around us. Is it any wonder He wants to do something special with our voices? So the body's response to the Spirit is to open this main gate of the voice, and "begin to speak" as the Holy Spirit gives the utterance.

Rita's brother, the well-known surgeon, Dr. William Standish Reed, defines this as "God's Spirit filling the area of speech," and another close friend of ours, Dr. Howard W. Dueker, leading neurosurgical specialist in the Los Angeles area, says, in effect, "The speech centers dominate the brain, and I don't see how God Himself could do much with the human brain unless He did something drastic with the speech centers!"

Because the ability to speak rationally is fundamental to being human, and profoundly important to our spiritual and psychological makeup, it seems to us that a complete "baptism in the Holy Spirit" in which our Lord, the Spirit, floods and fills our beings, and overflows to the outside world, will as a matter of course include allowing the Spirit greater freedom to guide our voices.

The Holy Spirit wants to tame the "unruly member" (James 3). He wants to show us how to use our voices properly. In Zephaniah 3:9 (RSV), there is a promise that God will "change the speech of the peoples to a pure speech, that all of them may call on the name of the Lord," and speaking in tongues may be seen as a fulfillment of this promise.

In the current renewal, millions would testify that it was when they began to "speak in tongues and magnify God" that new freedom came.

Pentecost issues from the Spirit of God in the re-created human spirit. Speaking in tongues is "praying by means of the Spirit,"[3] as Paul calls it (1 Cor. 14:15). It is not an emotional outburst, nor is it caused by emotion at all. If a person speaks in tongues emotionally, this is because the speaking in tongues is causing him to be moved by emotion, not because emotion is causing him to speak in tongues. You might become emotional while you were speaking English or French. For example, I was reading aloud to Rita from a very moving story, and I "choked up" with emotion, and was unable to go on reading for a while. I did not "get emotional" and so cause myself to read the story, I read the story and got emotional!

Speaking in tongues is simply what happens when a person who has received Jesus and, therefore, has been given the Holy Spirit, begins to speak without using the language the intellect knows, but trusts the Holy Spirit to give the words. It is a simple method by which the Holy Spirit opens us to new freedom and release. In everyday speaking we reach into the storehouse of words in our intellect—our computer—and select the ones we want. This is an activity of the soul, directed by the will. But now suppose instead of the will deciding what is to be said, it allows the spirit, united to the Holy Spirit, to provide the language? In this case all the *will* does is to

---

[3]All Christians "pray in the Spirit" when their prayer is guided by the Holy Spirit within them, no matter what language they pray in. However the only definition of "praying in the Spirit" we can find in the Scripture comes in reference to speaking in tongues (1 Corinthians 14:14). Perhaps this is because prayer in a known language "in the Spirit" means praying from mind and spirit combined, whereas praying in tongues is 100 percent "in the Spirit" since the mind does not understand what is being said.

accept the words as they come from the *spirit* and give them to the body's speech mechanism to be made into sounds.

The intellect is not providing the words. Paul, again, says "my mind is unfruitful" (1 Cor. 14:14), meaning that the words are not the "fruit" of the intellect. The intellect simply stands by, so to speak, and watches the process. The will is still in control. This is not compulsive or hypnotic activity. There is no taking-over of the will by the Holy Spirit. He always respects our freedom of choice.

Speaking in tongues is not some kind of achievement, or a proof of spirituality or holiness, but it can perform a specific and needed function daily in your life. Your spiritual freedom will increase because you are allowing the Holy Spirit to flow from your spirit, with the consent of your will, to guide you to express prayer and praise to God as the Holy Spirit inspires (Rom. 8:26, 27). Speaking in tongues is a wonderful instrument of the Spirit. It is the language of your spirit speaking to God.

We are still imperfect, and our souls contain a lot of things that need to be eliminated, so that we cannot with our own wills, intellects, and emotions speak or pray adequately. The Holy Spirit, by the use of a language that is unknown to our minds, puts into words exactly what God knows we need to express. It is a "pure language," just as God promised, because the soul doesn't understand it, and so can't mess it up! (Zeph. 3:9).

Difference Between Praying in Tongues
and the Gift of Tongues

Please be sure to note that the kind of "speaking by the Spirit" we have been talking about here is the private activity Paul describes when he says "I will pray with the spirit . . . I will praise with the spirit . . ." (1 Cor. 14:15). He goes on to add that when he is in a group situation he doesn't "speak in languages" but speaks with his understanding so that everyone can know what's being said (1 Cor. 14:19). We haven't so far been talking about the "gift of tongues" with its companion "gift of interpretation" that Paul refers to in 1 Corinthians 12:10.

Not everyone will be inspired to bring a gift of tongues in a meeting. In speaking in tongues as a prayer language, the decision to speak comes from the will, and the Holy Spirit honors that decision and provides the language; in the *gift* of tongues in a meeting, it is slightly different. Here the Holy Spirit initiates the desire to speak in tongues to meet a specific situation. The will must still give consent. As a result the language spoken in the gift of tongues may be quite different from that customarily used in daily praying in tongues.

Importance of Praying 100 Percent in the Spirit

It is our firm conviction that *any* Christian can pray and praise in a spiritual language at *any* time he or she decides to do so. St. Paul, again, says, *"thelo de pantas humas lalein glossais"*: "I want you all to speak in tongues" (1 Cor. 14:5). He says: "I thank God I speak in tongues more than any of you" (1 Cor. 14:18), or as it is in the original, "I thank my God, speaking in languages, more than all of you." In 1 Corinthians 14:15 Paul says: "I *will* pray with my spirit . . .," referring to speaking in tongues.

A woman who resisted the idea of speaking in tongues said to Rita, "After all, I have had *visions* from God, why should I want to speak with tongues?"

This question put Rita "on the spot" in a public meeting. She wanted to make a loving response, and yet be truthful. She quickly asked the Lord for help, and then answered, "That's wonderful to have visions from God, yet Peter did something even more dramatic than having visions, he walked on water! But on the day of Pentecost, Peter didn't say 'I don't need to speak in tongues. That's fine for my friends here, but you see I've walked on water!'"

Mary, the mother of Jesus, could certainly have said, "I've had the greatest experience of anyone, that of giving birth to the Son of God. Don't tell me *I* should speak in tongues," yet Mary, a truly humble person, willingly and joyfully on the day of Pentecost spoke with tongues along with the rest (Acts 1:14, 2:1ff).

You don't have to speak with tongues in order to be a faithful child of God. There are very shaky Christians who speak in tongues fluently, and very sincere and committed Christians who would do almost anything rather than speak in tongues, because they have been taught against it. Christians certainly don't have to speak in tongues in order to experience benefits from the Holy Spirit, or to manifest gifts of the Spirit such as healing, knowledge, and others. But what Jesus calls the "baptism" in the Spirit—the release, or outflow, of the Spirit—gives freedom of expression to the believer. This results in edification or being built up in your spirit, new ability to pray and intercede, and a greater openness to the flow of the gifts and fruit of the Holy Spirit. We are also becoming increasingly aware of how speaking in tongues can help heal the soul from past hurts, as people pray for their own infirmities—"praying in the Spirit" (Rom. 8:26).

Some Christians have relegated the prayer tongue to the least of God's gifts, like the bottom rung of a ladder. Our belief is there aren't any least or greater gifts, but the one needed at the moment becomes the "best" gift. Even if it *were* the bottom rung, what better place would there be for us to begin?

The Results

We thought you might be interested to see some of the results in our own personal lives after receiving the baptism in the Holy Spirit. Here is a composite list which applied to both of us:

1. A tremendously heightened sense of God's reality and presence.
2. An awareness of Jesus' love and closeness increased many times over.
3. A heightened appreciation and greater love for the Scriptures.
4. A greater desire to witness to others about Jesus and the power of the Holy Spirit, and to pray with them for both experiences.
5. A realization of what it means to praise God, and a new ability and desire to do it.
6. A greater love and concern for others.
7. A recognition of the gifts of the Spirit, and an awareness of them as such.
8. An appreciation of Christians of all denominations.
9. We began to have dreams about Jesus, and found ourselves acting like empowered believers even when asleep and dreaming. If threatened in our dreams we found ourselves praying or rebuking the enemy.
10. We realized the reality of the enemy, Satan, and what to do to steer clear of him, and how to take authority over him.

Rita experienced these additional benefits as well:

1. I had purpose and direction in my life for the first time.
2. I had a desire to forgive everybody and a willingness to ask forgiveness for myself from others.
3. I possessed a new discernment, and the power and confidence to pray for those in spiritual bondage.
4. I felt more confident in life after death, and a certainty of my ultimate safety and destination.
5. I became confident in giving a Christian witness in front of audiences.
6. I became interested in taking care of my physical body (temple) for God.
7. A new awareness in hearing the inner voice of God came to me.

Dennis also experienced additional benefits:

1. A great release of joy, freedom, and peace (fruit) even when things were a mess.
2. A realization that God is not "mystical," but here and now.
3. A new ease in preaching and teaching.
4. Greater sensitivity to the worship of my own church.
5. A loss of embarrassment in praying with people or talking with people about God.
6. A new ability and discernment in counseling.
7. A greater love for my family.

Would We Go Back?

If we had a choice, would we go back and live as Christians without the baptism in the Holy Spirit? Not on your life! Were we born again and on our way to heaven before this new freedom came along? Yes, of course, we were. Did we need Pentecost in our lives to become effective? Yes, because as you can see from our lists, we both had the experience of becoming much more effective in our respective ways following this experience. We can't speak for others, but this is the way it was for us. Most important, we began to enjoy God in a new way, and our joy flowed out to others.[4]

Jesus promised two things would happen as a result of the baptism in the Spirit: we would receive *power*, and we would be equipped to tell about Him at home and all over the world (Acts 1:8). He wants each of us to be that kind of witness.

[4]To help you pray for the baptism in the Spirit read *The Holy Spirit and You* by Dennis and Rita Bennett, Logos, 1971.

15

Ebb and Flow

And so the picture is completed. We receive Jesus, our sins are forgiven. Our spirits come alive by being joined to the Holy Spirit, and we become "new creatures." Then the new life is released in us to flow into our souls and bodies, and so out to the world "that the world may see that we are His disciples," and we live happily ever after!

No. Wait a minute. We began this book with a series of problems. There was Carol, and Bill, and Tony. They were all reborn in Christ, and had received the power of the Holy Spirit, yet they still had problems.

How about us—Dennis and Rita? In the previous chapter we listed some of the good things that happened in our lives after receiving the baptism in the Holy Spirit. Are all of these continuing undiminished? Unfortunately, no. Some things haven't changed, but most of them ebb and flow, and need to be renewed regularly. We often need correction and forgiveness, but we're learning. In fact this book is the product of some of the things we've been learning and, believe us, we've got a lot yet to learn!

Fortunately God is very patient and very kind!

We would like to keep the freedom we had when first released in the Spirit, while continuing to grow. Not "grow *up*," just *grow*. We're not supposed to grow *up* in the sense of losing our first childlike enthusiasm.[1] We're supposed to become wise children, keeping our enthusiasm and simplicity, while learning to be more stable and consistent in our trust in the Lord.

Would we want to go back to those first months of our Pentecost (Dennis, 1959; Rita, 1960)? No, because we know that we are learning how to remove the obstructions that have sometimes interfered with our freedom, and that when we do, we are going to have even more joy in the Lord than at first, plus the stability and knowledge we have gained. We wouldn't want to have to learn it all over again! Did you ever see the lapel button that displays the initials "PBPWMGINFWMY"? "Please be patient with me, God is not finished with me yet!"

Keeping the Overflow

You come to Christ at a particular time and place, and that's when your salvation begins. That's when the Holy Spirit comes to live in you. But it's only a beginning. When you ask Jesus into your life, He starts a process of rescuing, reclamation, feeding, teaching, healing, guiding, that will go on and on. The Greek word that is translated "save" in the Bible is *sozo*, and the Greek lexicon says it means to "preserve or rescue, bring out safely, save or free from disease, restore to health or keep in health, nurture, cause to thrive or prosper, save from eternal death."[2]

---

[1]In Ephesians 4:15 Paul does not say we are to "grow *up*" into Christ, but simply *grow* in or into Him. The "up" has been added by translators and paraphrasers. "Grow up" implies for us the attaining of adulthood or maturity, at which point we cease to grow. This is not what the original Greek says.

[2]William F. Arndt and F. Wilbur Gingrich, *A Greek-English Lexicon of the New Testament*, The University of Chicago Press (Grand Rapids, Mich.: Zondervan Publishing House, 1952).

Let's say you saw a man drowning in the river, and fished him out. You would have saved him, rescued him. But would you just say, "Okay, I saved you," and walk off and leave him shivering on the bank of the river? He might fall or jump right back in. You would certainly want to find out why he was in the river. *Did* he fall in? Was he thrown in? By whom? Was he trying to kill himself? The first thing you would do would be to get him a hot bath and some dry clothes, but you wouldn't stop there. You'd find out who he was and how you could help him. Does he need a job? Was he having home troubles? (You might have to help his wife and kids too!) All this would be a part of "saving" him. It might be a long assignment!

So the baptism in the Holy Spirit is really the continuation of Jesus' work in our lives, pouring out His love and power from where He is living in our spirits to continue to inspire, refresh, guide, renew and heal our souls and bodies, and out through us into the world to continue His redeeming work there. Just as when we receive Jesus as Savior we are beginning a new kind of life in which He will continue to work with us every moment, so the baptism in the Holy Spirit is supposed to be a continuing flow of life. Ephesians 5:18 in the original language says "be being filled with the Holy Spirit"— "keep on being filled," to which we would add "keep on overflowing."

What Prevents It From Continuing?

What interrupts the flow? Unless we see the distinction between spirit and soul, we won't have much chance to discover what keeps us from moving ahead in the Spirit. The person who sees himself or herself as only twofold will have no way to explain why he or she should lose freedom except to say (1) "I guess the Lord must have left me, and I need to get Him back," or (2) "My body is the culprit."

If we are made up of only two parts—a "spiritual nature" and a "physical nature," one or the other must be at fault. If, however, you see that between your spirit and your body there is the area of the soul, you can also see that this is the real battleground.

We have shown how the soul tries to be something in its own right that it was never meant to be: the emotions that get away from the true feelings of the spirit; the will that has its own plans and ambitions; the intellect that becomes devoted to itself—what we can call intellectual-*ism*. The soul needs to be put back into the role it was made for, but it strongly resists the process.

The Apostle Paul refers to the soul when it's trying to run things as the "old man" (Rom. 6:6). He says that this old man was crucified, put out of action, when Jesus died on the cross. The old man was crucified, but the patterns he established are still there in the soul and need to be corrected. This is why Satan finds the soul such a satisfactory hunting ground. He knows just where to irritate and stir you up. He knows just what buttons to push to get the results he wants!

You know how it goes. You're doing just fine, sailing along with the Lord, and at peace with mankind, and then the enemy touches your *emotions* in a sensitive spot: "Do you know what Jackie said about you down at the office?"

"Gr-r-r-r!" Away goes your blessing, as the emotion of fear, anger, or jealousy is stirred up in your soul.

Or Satan drops a question to the *intellect:* "Did God create the world in six days, or did He take billions of years?" "Is the Bible 'verbally inerrant' or not?" "How do you interpret Ezekiel 38?" "How can you convince your agnostic friend that there is a God?" And if you're not careful, you lose track of your joy while you're struggling to find the answers. Someone said, "Don't stone the devil's dogs, and don't chase the devil's rabbits," but it's hard to resist them when he runs them across the trail!

Or Satan says to the *will:* "You've got to accomplish something. Try harder; you're number two! You've got to make something of yourself. This religion business is all very well, but what about your plans and ambitions for your everyday life?" Or he says, "You really should make some more good resolutions!"

When the soul is ruling, if someone hurts you, your natural reaction is to hurt them back, only worse. The soul is great at defending itself, trying to get its rights. The Holy Spirit in us, if we are listening, will have us give back good for evil, blessing for cursing. But the patterns in the soul are so strong that we may forget to listen to the Spirit, and just react from emotion, will, and intellect.

"We have been working from time to time with the men in a nearby federal penitentiary," says Dennis, "and I met a young man there who'd been in a good deal of trouble, but like many of the fellows, had accepted Jesus and been baptized in the Spirit, and his life was totally changed. On this day, however, he said to me, 'I don't know what's wrong, Father Bennett; I seem to be losing out with the Lord. I just don't have the joy and love I did. I seem to be getting back into some of those old thoughts and feelings.' "

"What have you been doing lately?" Dennis inquired, and the young man explained he had been taking courses at a nearby college, on a special program that allowed prisoners to do this. As he talked about it, his face clouded. "And I've got this professor—he sure makes me mad! He's always talking against Christianity. But I argue with him. I really give him a bad time!"

"M-m-m," Dennis responded. "And there's your problem! You're getting so involved in your soul with opposing this prof that you're forgetting to love and forgive him from the spirit. Your will is determined to put him down, your intellect is busy tackling the questions he raises, and your emotions are being upset by the whole thing. Stop trying to give him a bad time. As the Holy Spirit gives you the answers, continue to challenge the prof but forgive and love him, too. You are much more likely to convince him that way."

What Is the Flesh?

Jesus said, "Watch and pray so that you don't get tempted: the spirit indeed is willing, but the *flesh* is weak" (Matt. 26:41b). Here's a little different term: the *flesh*. What does this mean? The word in Greek is *sarx*. It is used in two ways in the Scripture, one is to describe the physical body. In this sense it is certainly not a bad, but a good thing. Speaking of Jesus' body, John 1:14 says: "The Word became flesh *(sarx)*. . . ." When God had made human flesh for the first time He said, "It is very good!" (Gen. 1:31).

The second meaning of "flesh" refers not only to the body, but to the body and the soul function-ing on their own, not obeying God. Thus in Gala-tians 5:19 we have a list of the "doings of the flesh," and it doesn't just include things like sexual sins and drunkenness which we associate with the body, but also idolatry, sorcery, hatred, ill-will, anger, selfishness, envy, all of which are clearly in the soul. (Of course drunkenness or adultery are also from the body, but the body wouldn't of itself do these things.) So the main component of the "flesh" is certainly the soul. This is also what Paul means by the "carnal" man. Carnal is from late Latin *carnalis* meaning "of the flesh."

Where Are You Living?

It's important to know the difference between soul and spirit,[3] because the spirit is the only part of you that can contact God. You can't *think, emote,* or *will* your way to God.

Understanding the difference makes it possible to check our spiritual thermometers to see what's ruling our lives. Ask yourself: "Is this situation causing anxiety, turmoil, hate, unrest, or is it bringing me peace, confidence, assurance, understanding, love? Am I living in my soul or in my spirit?

The baptism in the Spirit provides much more power and ability for the spirit to subdue the soul, but the will still has the choice, and subliminal influences and patterns of the old life can still interfere, and need to be dealt with day by day. This is, again, why Paul can on the one hand say that his old man was crucified (Rom. 6:6, literal Greek), but on the other that he needs to "die daily"—die, that is, to the patterns left behind by the old man! So, in the light of the picture of spirit, soul, and body—the triune person—let's look at some of the blocks and barriers that need to be cleared.

---

[3]To grasp the distinction between soul and spirit in the Scripture, it's helpful to notice the way in which the Greek words *psuche* and *pneuma* are used in the New Testament. Unfortunately many translations and paraphrases tend to overlook the difference. The King James Version is one of the most accurate, although it is not consistent in capitalization, so that one can only presume from the context, in some passages, whether the writer is referring to the spirit of man or the Spirit of God.

Even if you cannot read Greek (and most people can't) you can get hold of a copy of an Interlinear Greek New Testament, which runs a literal English translation right beneath each Greek word. With an elementary knowledge of the Greek alphabet, you can quickly learn to recognize which of the two words is being used.

16

How the Will Can Block the Spirit

"You know, you can make a barn door fly if you apply enough power," says a friend who helps design airplanes for Boeing in Seattle. Some of us were pretty rough and dilapidated barn doors, with very little streamlining, but when the Holy Spirit turned on the afterburners, we took off! We may have crashed after a while, but we sure did *fly*! It's the engines that would make the barn door fly, even though it is a very poor airfoil, with lots of form drag. If the engines are producing plenty of power, it will help if we streamline the barn door a bit and get rid of some of the roughness, but if the engines aren't working, it won't do a bit of good. So let's not make the mistake of thinking that the first and most important consideration is correcting the malformations of the barn door. The first job is to keep the engines going, because if a flying barn door is the best we can do, a barn door in the air is better than a 747 on the ground with inoperative engines!

There are a lot of Christians who don't know anything about the differences between "spirit, soul, and body," or the need to get the hurts in their souls healed in order to fly more efficiently, but they're *flying*! They may perform some pretty odd maneuvers from time to time, and frighten the other folks around, but they're airborne, and things are happening. This was certainly true of some of the heroes and heroines of the early days of Pentecost, and it is true of some still on the scene today. They may lack finesse, and may seem to lack understanding in some ways. They may be turning some people off by their antics, but because they are open and willing, and love the Lord, He is able to work through them anyway. It would be better if they were *both* power-packed *and* streamlined, but if we have to choose, we'll choose the power, and pick up the pieces!

In this book we are, among other things, trying to show how we can make *our* flying machines more effective and airworthy, but let's remember that means we must give attention to both our aerodynamic cleanness—the correcting of blocks in soul and body—*and* our source of power, the nurturing and strengthening of the Spirit's outflow.

Having done our best to be sure the power is flowing, we are ready to give our attention to streamlining.

After human beings were cut off from God spiritually, and the soul had taken command, the will could no longer look to the spirit for guidance, so was forced to make its own decisions from the data supplied by the intellect, the emotions, and the bodily senses. This meant that the will had to decide on the bases of *reasoning, feeling,* and *reacting* to events in the outside world.

Your Way or His Way

As long as people are spiritually separated from God, the only way God can give any guidance is by establishing law and principles for the *will* to operate by. This is the way things were in the Old Testament. After a person has been reborn of the Spirit, and is back in touch with God, it's difficult for the *will* to make the transition to the "new and living way" of the New Testament in which God wants to guide us directly through our fellowship with Him in the Holy Spirit. The will still wants just to *modify* its own plans to make them line up with God's will; basically the human will still wants to do what it wants to do. It isn't direct rebellion; it's more subtle than that. It's turning to *legalism*—"You tell me what the rules are, Lord, and I'll obey and fit my plans into them, and thus earn your approval."

It's what the children of Israel did at Sinai. They said to Moses, "You go up and talk to God, and tell us what He wants us to do. Anything He says for us to do, we'll do it!" (Exod. 19:8.)

Jesus says, "I'll be with you always. Trust Me, and I'll guide you."

Then the will says, "Isn't that great? Jesus will go with *me* and help me carry out *my* plans. Come on, Lord. I've got some great ideas!"

A little later we say, "Lord, I thought you were going to be with me? Look at the mess I'm in!"

The Lord answers: "Correction—look at the mess *we're* in! I'm *with* you, remember? I don't like this situation either. But we wouldn't be in this mess if you had come with Me where I wanted to take you. You have been insisting that I go with you where *you* wanted to go; and that's just where we are! Now start following *Me* and we'll get things in order!"

People get turned off, and even disillusioned with God because their plans, which seemed so worthy, haven't worked out. They didn't really let God into those plans, though. They just expected Him to bless whatever *they* had decided to do! Have you noticed how amazingly well things work out and fit together when you are allowing God to guide you instead of trying to fulfill obligations and "get things done" as *you* have planned?

Frustrated by Plan B?

Then there's *frustration*. The will wants to decide on a course of action, but can't do so, or it wants to take a certain direction but is stopped by circumstances it cannot control. This, again, is the result of not looking to the Holy Spirit for guidance. If you are expecting the Holy Spirit to show you the way, you won't be frustrated if things seem contradictory. You'll just wait until the Lord clears it up. And if there is opposition to what seems to be obviously the right plans, you won't be frustrated by that either; you'll wait for the Lord to remove the opposition, or to give you plan "B."

There is a very subtle way in which the enemy tries to get us to stop trusting God. It works like this. You are trying to make a decision: let's say you are trying to decide whether to resign from your job and accept one in another community. You try to get guidance from the Lord, and He seems to be leading you to go ahead. All the doors open. You find housing easily and reasonably in the new community. You find someone who will move your belongings reasonably; the new job seems to fit you just right. Everything is going like clockwork, and then, after you have quit your old job, and are ready for the move, something goes wrong. Someone at the new business objects to your coming, or the opening you had planned on filling is suddenly closed due to realignment of the organization, or the man who was going to buy your old house backs out of the deal, etc., etc. What now? Did God let you down? You were trying to follow His leading, and now look what's happened!

Ah, but wait a minute. You were trying to follow His leading, but you were still thinking of it as *God* telling you what to do, and *you* carrying it out on your own. You forgot again that He is *with* you in the situation. When the door closed in your face, it closed in *His* face too! He isn't just sitting up in heaven pulling strings; He's with you and in you. He's on your side always (Rom. 8:31). Don't panic, just ask Him to activate "Plan B"!

We forget that God cannot force people to do what He wants them to do without taking away their freedom, which He will not do. In *The Spiritual Man* Watchman Nee writes that neither God nor the devil can do anything with us without first obtaining consent—"for man's will is free."[1] God intended the person in the new organization to say "yes" to your coming, but he said "no." Therefore a human being can check God Himself by saying "no" when God had planned for him or her to say "yes," and so cause "Plan A" to fail. But God always has "Plan B"! (And "C," and "D," and as many as are needed!)

Satan loves to push us into frustration: "You *must* make up your mind," he urges. "You must take action. You'll miss the opportunity." But God always knows the perfect timing.

You Take the First Step

God doesn't want us to *give up* our wills. Many times you hear people talk as though God wanted to crush our wills. Usually it is said that He wants to "break" us. This is an unfortunate word, as it normally implies some kind of

---

[1]Watchman Nee, *The Spiritual Man* (Great Britain: The Chaucer Press, Ltd., Bungay, Suffolk).

destruction. God gave us freedom of will so that we could decide to follow Him, not from fear, or from a desire to earn rewards or merits, but for love's sake.

He doesn't want to "break" our wills in the sense of destroying them, but in the sense in which we "break" a horse from its wild state to become a usable and workable creature. Even this is a less than happy example, for God does not desire to drive us like horses. Perhaps a better picture would be that of a polo pony, who enters into the game almost as much as his rider does. God wants us freely to pattern our wills after His, to let the Holy Spirit in us conform our will to His so we will want the same thing He wants because His nature is in us. It's still a free choice.

For us just to obey God, by suppressing our own desires, would be like the little boy who was standing up on the pew in church. "Sit down, son," said his daddy, but the boy remained standing.

"I said sit down," repeated the father, but this time he put his hand on the boy's shoulder and gently but firmly pushed him into a sitting position. The child looked at his dad and announced, "I'm sitting down on the outside, but I'm standing up on the inside!"

We may need to restrain ourselves sometimes, that's true, and do things we really don't want to do because we know God wants us to do them, but if we never get any farther than doing God's wishes because we want approval or rewards, or just because we fear punishment, where's the joy in that? Ultimately God not only wants us to want what He wants, but thoroughly to enjoy doing it, because we love Him, and He loves us.

Some people have said things like: "All that abundant living in Christ sounds fine for others, but I'm just too weak to manage it. I'm a weak-willed person." Rita was pondering this one day, when she remembered the experience Jesus had with the Gadarene man who had been taken over completely—or so it seemed—by a legion of demons (Luke 8:26ff). The man seemed totally "out of it." He'd torn off all his clothes, and cut his body. They couldn't even chain him up, because he would break the chains. Yet when this person saw Jesus, he ran to Him and fell at His feet. All the legion of demons that were tormenting him couldn't stop him because he *willed* to come to the Lord for help.

Then a thought came to Rita from the Holy Spirit: "The weakest will in the world is strong enough to turn to Jesus." No one reading this is as bad off as the Gadarene! No matter how weak you may feel—you're never too weak to call on Jesus for help.

Your will is more powerful than your feelings or your memories. If you take that first little step and say, "Jesus help me," He will always respond to your call.

17

Blocks and Blessings
of the Intellect

"Garbage in, garbage out"—is a proverb with those who work with computers. You've got to ask a computer the right questions, program it correctly, and interpret the results properly if you want more than garbage. The same thing is true of the computers we carry around in our skulls, our amazing brains. Your brain is not your intellect, but is a most important instrument used by your intellect.[1] Your intellect includes the way you handle your thinking machine: it's the whole process of reasoning and it's wonderful. God gave it to you to use.

The intellect becomes a block to the spirit, however, when it fails to grasp the difference between spirit and soul and insists that it must understand *everything*, not just its own affairs, but those of the spirit, too, and even of the Holy Spirit. "I'm not going to accept anything I can't understand or reason out!" In the first part of the book Tony Carter was having a struggle with his intellect, you remember, because he was insisting on grasping every-

[1]Dr. H.W. Dueker, neurosurgeon, from Van Nuys, California, puts it something like this: "We can trace the physical locations of will, emotion, and intellect in the human brain. We may reasonably say that the brain represents the machinery of the soul, but one need not entertain the idea that the brain *is* the soul."

thing first and foremost with his mind.

In the realm of the spirit, however, the intellect needs to step back and humbly say, "This is out of my territory. It transcends my ability to understand and explain." When this happens, there is no conflict, and the intellect can take its place as the handmaid of the Spirit.

If you see the difference between soul and spirit, you see that as long as you are operating with the soul, you can expect to understand things with your head, but when you move into the realm of the spirit, although you are still not denying reason and don't have to be irrational, you have moved into the area *above* the rational, the *super*-rational.

> Reason has moons, but moons not hers
> Lie mirrored on her sea,
> Confounding her astronomers,
> But O! delighting me.[2]

The Use of the Bible

Dr. Dueker, whom we've already quoted, had this to say one day: "My favorite kind of Bible study is not only when I gain intellectual knowledge about the Bible, but when God seems to bypass my intellect and speak directly to my spirit."

Jesus said: "It is the Spirit that quickens; the flesh profits nothing: the words that I speak to you are spirit, and they are life" (John 6:63, KJV modernized). When Jesus speaks to us from the pages of Scripture, they transmit His life to our spirits. We can sometimes feel a quickening within us, and that means growth. We agree that this is the greatest kind of Bible study, when God's Spirit speaks directly to our spirits (John 4:24).

[2]Ralph Hodgson, "Reason." *Familiar Quotations*, Bartlett, 1943, p. 816.

The words of Jesus found in the four Gospels should thus be the foundation for all Bible reading. From there we go to the Acts of the Apostles, the letters of Paul and others, then to the rest of the Bible. Jesus can quicken these other parts of the Scripture to us as we look to find Him revealed in them (Luke 24:27-32).

Another friend, Mary Burbank, asked this question: "How does Scripture feed our spirits? Does it first inspire our minds, and then move from mind to spirit? Or does it go directly from Spirit to spirit, and then from spirit to mind?" We think the answer is "both ways." As we meditate intellectually on the Scripture, the Holy Spirit can bring it alive to our spirits. It seems to come most purely and powerfully though when God's Spirit speaks directly to ours.

The Holy Spirit can speak directly to the human spirit, without having to explain things to the intellect. There is an inner knowing of the spirit, that completely transcends the calculations of the soul. The people were amazed at Jesus. "This man speaks with authority," they said, "not like the scribes" (Mark 1:22, et al.). Jesus didn't have to quote anyone else to back Him up, because the Holy Spirit confirmed the truth of what He was saying for those who had ears to hear. He was teaching in the Spirit, not only by the intellect.

Biblical Intellectualism

The Apostle James tells us to "receive with humility the implanted Word which has the power to save and nurture our souls" (James 1:21). Here he is rather clearly *not* speaking primarily of Scripture, but of Jesus, the Word, whose life has been implanted in our spirits by our being joined to the Holy Spirit. All through this book, we've been talking about "receiving the implanted Word"—allowing the life of God living in us to flow out and transform our souls and bodies to become more like Jesus.

It is not the Bible—the physical book—that "saves our souls." The Holy Spirit uses the words of the Scripture to speak directly to us. The Bible is His special book because it contains the inspired record of God's dealings with man in the past. It is the supreme book of testimony and guidance.

We need to understand the Bible intellectually, too, as much as we can, but this is a road strewn with all kinds of pitfalls. It's possible to be a "biblical intellectualist." In the last couple of hundred years, scholars began to study the Bible purely intellectually, and the result has been a kind of destructive criticism which in its most extreme form reduces the Bible to the status of "just another book" of religious speculation and mythology, valuable only because of its moral teachings, and even these are being eliminated by the ultramodernists. On the other hand, many Christians reacted with another kind of intellectualism, approaching the Bible in a way that has led to interminable argument about its accuracy and infallibility, and sometimes to a kind of book-worship that can be just as cold and lifeless as the cleverness of the scribes and Pharisees in Jesus' day.

Jesus had great respect for the Scripture, but did not hesitate to point out that *He,* and not the book, is the source of life. "You don't have His Word living in you, because you don't believe Him whom He sent. Search the Scriptures, for in them you think you have eternal life, but they tell about *Me;* and you won't come to *Me* so that you can have life" (John 5:38-40). The intellect always wants to have something impersonal and objective to study whether it's a book, or a theory, or a physical object. The spirit knows better, and always seeks the living Word, Jesus, to enjoy fellowship with Him.

This is why the most effective use of the Bible is not just as the subject for intellectual study and discussion (although there is a time and place for that too) but to let the Holy Spirit speak directly to our spirits and then to our intellects.

The Holy Spirit will handle Scripture pretty freely! A friend of ours, J.A. Dennis of Austin, Texas, tells how the Lord gave him a promise of healing for his digestive system, "I will take sickness away from the midst of thee" (Exod. 23:25). He tells how a scholarly friend laughed at him, *"That* isn't what that text means at all!" "But," says our brother, "that's what it means *to me."* It worked. His stomach ulcer was healed.

Pride and Backwards Pride

The intellect is very vulnerable to pride. Intellectual pride leads a person to hang on to what he has figured out, or thinks he has figured out, even in the face of contrary facts. Scientists are as bad as theologians when it comes to this! Battles over scientific theories have been almost as cruel as the Inquisition. Go back and read about the difficulties faced by those who discovered oxygen, or the circulation of the blood, or who proposed the germ theory of disease, for example. It is so difficult for human beings really to be objective. Once the intellect has grasped something, it is very unwilling to let go.

There's another subtle intellectual trap, which can fool us because it looks very "spiritual," and that is to say, "Oh, I don't bother with all that doctrine stuff, that's just a 'head trip.' I just follow the Lord!" This is a backwards kind of intellectual pride, pride in *not* using your head!

The catch is that it is impossible not to use your head. Everyone forms some kind of theory or idea about God—a theology, and if you don't get a good theology, you'll surely get a bad one! The human intellect is going to find answers one way or another. So don't think you're not supposed to use your head when it comes to spiritual things. It's just you need to recognize the limitations of the intellect in the world of the Spirit.

Doubt Never Arrives

Doubt is a good attitude, again, in the scientific field. A good investigator will doubt everything, and will never say, "I know for sure." Scientists don't talk about "laws," just theories, and a theory can be overthrown at any time if new facts come down the line. Doubt never arrives, although it may draw closer to its goal. It always says, like the old song, "Till the real thing comes along, I'll string along with you!"

Spiritual life, on the other hand, begins with absolute confidence, not in a set of facts, but in a person, and proceeds from there. In science, one's judgment should be reserved at all times, but in faith, the mind is made up once and for all. Faith *begins* with commitment; in fact, spiritually, doubt is precisely the opposite of faith. The great St. Augustine, Bishop of Hippo, put things in the right order when he said, *"Credo, ut intelligam,"* "I believe in order that I may understand."

Doubt can be an emotional matter too. I'm doubtful because I am fearful, or I'm doubtful because I am influenced by the personality of some other person. Doubt leads to double-mindedness, and the Scripture says a "double-minded man is unstable in all his ways" (James 1:8). Jesus told us not to be "of doubtful mind" (Luke 12:29). He said, "If you have faith, and don't doubt . . .

you shall say to this mountain, be removed and thrown into the sea, and it shall be done" (Matt. 21:21). And in Mark 11:23 He says that the person who does not "doubt in his heart, . . . shall have whatsoever he says."

Misinformation

There is another trap for the intellect, and that is *mis*information. "A little learning is a dangerous thing," is Alexander Pope's often quoted line.

If you aren't willing really to dig into a subject, you should not rely on your knowledge of that subject. In science each researcher builds on the work of the one before him or her. No progress would be made if each had to repeat and verify all the experiments and thinking already done. In the field of religion, on the other hand, especially in times of renewal, there is a tendency to reject or ignore what has been said and thought in the past. Don't be an "instant expert" on spiritual matters. Do read and listen to what others have said in the past, and are saying in the present.

Someone has said, "A theologian must think in centuries." This means he or she can say to you: "I wouldn't follow that idea if I were you. Three hundred years ago a group of people adopted that idea, and they went over the cliff, right over there!"

"I went down to the supermarket to buy an outdoor thermometer," says Dennis. "I looked at several dozen of them lying in the bin, and they all seemed to be reading a little differently! At first I was going to give up, since the instruments were all so inaccurate. Then I got a bright idea. I laid about a dozen of the thermometers side by side, averaged their readings, and picked one that read the average."

None of us understand God perfectly, that is why we

must compare our "readings" with those around us, and also with those who have lived and died before us.

What Are the Cures?

What then, in summary, are the cures for blocks in the intellect? First, not to reject the intellect, but on the other hand not to take it too seriously. Realize that the intellect is a very useful tool of the soul, and important in helping us live in this world, but that in the world of the Spirit, the intellect must take a very humble place. This is one of the reasons the Holy Spirit gives us the manifestation of praying by or in the Spirit. "If I pray in a language, [tongue] my spirit prays," says Paul. "My *mind* [intellect] is unfruitful" (1 Cor. 14:14). Speaking in the Spirit is one of the clearest and most direct evidences that the spirit can function directly without the intellect having to "get in on the act." When someone is speaking in tongues, the will is very much involved, but the intellect for the moment is the least necessary item!

A Franciscan monk we met in Germany had just begun to speak in tongues. He complained to us "Ach! This is the humiliation of my intellect!" It's hard for the soul to yield to the Spirit, but so very important.

Secondly, to realize that we should train our intellects well in the area of our faith. We need to understand all we can about how men and women have experienced God, and interpreted the Scripture. We need to be able to think logically about the things of God, as long as we realize that God may transcend (not contradict) our logic. God does not contradict Himself; He invented logic!

The third, and most important thing to realize is that the intellect is at home in the area of the soul, but that in the world of the Spirit it is transcended, for "we have the mind of Christ" (1 Cor. 2:16b).

18

Feelings That Help and Hinder

Did you ever watch a crowd at a closely contested ball game? It's quite acceptable to shout, jump around, slap a perfect stranger on the back, groan, or even weep at crucial times. Would you want to coach a ball club with no emotion expressed from the bleachers? Do you notice how much more difficult it is for a team to win games when they are away than when feeling the warm backing of their fans at home?

Would you want to run a sales program, teach school, raise kids, make a speech, play golf, read a book, or do any of a thousand other things, without *emotion*? With no feeling? Emotion is vital.

If you were never moved by anything, you'd be dead! Or might just as well be! You can't *guide* your life by your emotions, and there are times when you must ignore your feelings, and just plug ahead with what you know is right. Yet even though you may walk in the dark for a while feeling-wise, you are looking forward to coming out into the light and experiencing love and joy and goodness. It would be too bad (if it were possible) to arrive in heaven, but still feel like hell! Heaven will be heaven for us not because of the surroundings (though they'll be pretty nice, too!), nor even just because God is *there*, but because we will be *responding* to God in love and joy—because we will *feel* and enjoy His presence.

Effect of Negative Emotions

The battle in the *emotions* is always between whether we will respond to the *world* around, or to the *Spirit* within. If the emotions are left to themselves, they will be swayed by the strongest impression of the moment. You know people who are up in the clouds when they are in happy Christian fellowship. Their spirits are being stirred and their emotions are responding to the Holy Spirit. But the next day, at the office, the strongest stimuli are coming from the environment—the pressures of the job—their emotions respond to them, and so they are upset, or depressed.

We Bennetts have learned, when we are getting ready to go on an important assignment, to look out for the enemy's tricks. He will, if possible, create situations in which emotions get disturbed. He will try to stir up some petty irritation—get us arguing, even mildly, on some unimportant matter. Or he will see to it that our baggage is delayed. He may try to stir up resentment if an airline employee is unhelpful or discourteous (which rarely happens), "They can't *do* this to me!", and so make us less ready to function in the Spirit. This is the emotion of anger.

Can anger ever be a response to the Spirit? Yes, there is such a thing as "righteous indignation," but it's *never* a hatred of people or things, only of the work of the enemy. Any time we feel a resentment or anger toward people or circumstances as such, we may be sure we are reacting to the world, and not responding to the Spirit. The fruit of the Spirit is love, joy, peace, no matter what is happening outside us. We aren't responsible for what others may do, but we are responsible for our reactions to their behavior. The Holy Spirit in us may stir us to action, but He will never upset us or make us feel confused and frustrated. We're not even allowed to rage at the devil! (Jude 9).

God will never make us *afraid*, either. The "fear of the Lord" is much misunderstood. It means of course "awe," not fright. There is a beautiful scene in that great children's classic, *The Wind in the Willows*: the mole and the water rat have just come upon Pan, in a woodland glade. He is a "Christ figure" to the animals in the story. They are gazing at him in adoration. Mole says, "Ratty, are you afraid?" The rat replies, "Afraid? Of him? Never! And yet, O mole, I am afraid!"

Human fear is the most deadly of the emotions, and the most destructive. It is, according to the Scripture, the opposite of love. "Perfect love casts out fear because fear has torment" (1 John 4:18). When walking in the Spirit we will never be afraid, because we are so aware of the guidance and love of God. Whenever we feel the emotion of fear we know that our emotions are responding to the world, and not the Spirit, and of course the ability of the Holy Spirit to move through our lives is then blocked very firmly. You can't respond to God when you are filled with fear.

Good Emotions Can Also Interfere

But it isn't only the unpleasant emotions that can interfere with the Spirit's work. There are some pleasant feelings that can do so too. Take affection. Affection is certainly an important emotion. Second Timothy 3:3 points out one of the signs of the breakdown of things in the last days will be that some are "without natural affection." It is good and natural for a child to feel affection for his parents, and vice versa. It is natural for a person to feel affection for the place of his birth, and for his or her friends. These are good things, but they, too, can get in the way of the Spirit, unless they are under His direction.

Jesus said not only that He had come to put a man at odds with his family (Matt. 10:35), but even that His followers had to "hate" father and mother (Luke 14:26). It is obvious from the Scripture that our Lord was not speaking literally, for He certainly did not hate His own mother, but showed tender concern for her. Yet when His mother and brothers came to persuade Him to give up His ministry, He said, "Who is my mother, and who are my brothers? . . . whoever does the will of my Father which is in heaven, is my brother, and sister, and mother" (Matt. 12:48-50).

The word "affection" deals with how something affects us. And this again can come from either direction, from God or from "the flesh." We can let God's love "affect" us and we can feel affection for Him. God's love in us will then make us able to feel affection toward our fellow humans, whether they are loveable or not, and whether they respond to us or not. This is the *agape* love the New Testament talks about, which loves because it has love in itself, not because the other person is necessarily loveable or lovely. It's God's kind of love.

Human affection, on the other hand, is exclusive. It loves one and not another, therefore it can create anger and jealousy. The Apostle Paul says to "set your affection on things above, not on things on the earth" (Col. 3:2) He isn't condemning human love and affection. It's quite clear that Paul had great affection for his friends—he speaks of it often. What he means is that even our human affection should come through God and be directed by God. Otherwise we're back with original sin, each person grasping and saying, "This is *mine!*"

Excitement and joy can also get in the way of the Spirit. We can be so taken up with jubilation over something good that has happened to us, that we can forget where our real joy and security is, and how transitory human joy is.

As we said already, all of these conscious emotions can be controlled. We sometimes have a hard time believing so, but they can. We can control our emotions by controlling our thoughts (intellect) and, of course, we control our thoughts by our wills. We can choose whether just to *react* to the things in the world around us, or whether we are going to *act* according to the inspiration of the Holy Spirit. I may think that such-and-such a person irritates me, but what actually happens is that I allow myself to be irritated; in fact, as one psychologist pointed out, I irritate *myself* when that person is around!

Emotions Which Try to Control Us

It is when we come to irrational and unconscious emotions that we find things we are unable to control. We can control how we act in response to these feelings, but we are unable to control the feelings directly.

Bill Carter, in the first chapter of this book, was having trouble with his affections. He was happily married, yet found himself tempted to flirt with the girls at the office. He controlled this inclination by his will, but it still troubled him. Why did he feel this way at all? For a while, after he had first received the freedom of the Holy Spirit, the feelings seemed to have gone, but then they returned.

It is simply cruel and silly to criticize a person such as Bill for having unacceptable *feelings*. Those feelings may be coming from areas of the person's emotional makeup that are currently out of his or her reach. If the person *acts out* the feelings, they are in trouble, because the behavior dictated by their feelings may be destructive and debilitating both to the individual and to society.

A man with a bad temper cannot be criticized for having the bad temper, but if he loses his temper, he's in trouble. It isn't a sin to *have* wrong feelings, but it *is* wrong to entertain them and let them control us or manifest through us.

Let's talk about how to get such *feelings* healed.

19

The Subconscious

Next to John 3:16, "God so loved the world. . .,"
perhaps the next best known Scripture would be
Revelation 3:20: "Behold, I stand at the door, and knock:
if any man hear my voice and open the door, I will come in
to him, and will sup with him, and he with me."

Millions of people have been reborn into the kingdom
by applying these words personally and inviting Jesus in,
to have fellowship with them in their spirits. Millions
more will be drawn to Him by this invitation.

However, when you look at the original context it's a
bit of a surprise to realize that Jesus isn't talking to
unbelievers but to believers. It's another example of the
Holy Spirit using the same Scripture in different ways. So
there's no quarrel with using Revelation 3:20 to lead
people to receive Jesus, but it's important for those who've
already received Him to see that in this passage He is
specifically talking to *them*.

What "door" then is Jesus knocking at? A believer has
already opened the door of his *spirit*, and the Lord has

come in. This must be referring to the door that leads to the *soul*. But again, when you receive the baptism in the Holy Spirit, as we've been trying to show in this book, you give Jesus greater access to your soul. If these people to whom Jesus is talking in the book of Revelation hadn't yet opened their souls, they weren't yet baptized in the Holy Spirit. That doesn't seem too likely. We know the church of Ephesus was Spirit-filled, yet Jesus was knocking at their doors too (Rev. 2:1-5). Are there other "doors" at which Jesus could be knocking, even in Spirit-filled Christians?

If a friend comes to visit, you let him or her into your house, but not necessarily into your *whole* house. When you receive Jesus, you let Him come and live in the "inner sanctuary" of your house, your spirit, and at times sense His touch in soul and body also. When you are baptized in the Holy Spirit, you let Him into the "working areas" of your house—kitchen, dining room, etc., and also begin to let His light shine out through your windows, and go out through the doors into the world around. But you can still have many doors shut to Him—doors to cupboards and closets, basement rooms and storage areas.

Shirley Shares a Dream

Sometimes God will give a recurring dream to help one of His children realize the unhealed memories which have been stuffed into the subconscious.

We were holding a mission in an Episcopal parish in Jacksonville, Florida. Shirley Tartt, a petite woman in her thirties, told us of a dream she had been having which had recurred the night before our meeting.

"In my dream I'm in a two-story house with many rooms," she said. "I'm going freely from room to room, dancing and happy. There's a room in the basement, though, that's dark and scary—there's a monster in it! As long as I stay away from the basement, I'm okay. God's done so many neat things for me already," Shirley went on, "but I think this dream is telling me there's an area of my life that still needs healing. What do you think?" She turned to Rita.

Rita thought a moment and then responded, "Were you ever locked in a room when you were a child?"

Shirley was silent, then she replied, "Why, yes. I remember when I was eight years old, in the orphanage in which I was brought up, some of the other kids accidentally locked me in a closet." She looked surprised as she went on, "Oh, another scene I had forgotten (repressed) comes to my mind. When I was fourteen I was locked in the cold storage room off the kitchen, only this time a girl did it on purpose." She paused again and continued, "Oh, yes, and that same girl held me under water in the swimming pool one day till I thought I was going to drown for sure!"

The meaning of that scary room in the basement of Shirley's dream was becoming more obvious. We prayed about each scene with her beginning with the least frightening one. She wrote later to say, "I'm praising God for setting me free from these situations which contributed to my fears so long ago. Even though I've had victory since the baptism with the Spirit (I used to be afraid to ride in an elevator), He apparently wanted these memories totally dealt with as only He can do. His perfect love truly casts out fear."

The Subconscious

The subconscious or unconscious is that area in your

soul where every experience you've had is stored away in computer-like memory banks. Everything you've seen, thought, felt, and sensed, from your conception to the present moment is there. It would be impossible to keep everything in your active memory so it is "warehoused" in the unconscious. Your subconscious contains all the feelings, thoughts, motivations, that have been recorded through your life. It's been compared to an iceberg. The tip that shows is the conscious part; but like the iceberg, the part under water is seven times larger.

There isn't much doubt about the existence of the unconscious mind, but opinions differ as to what part it plays. Some think God comes into the soul by way of the unconscious. Some would say the unconscious *is* the spirit.

We don't believe this is the right way to look at it. God does not enter the personality through the depths of the unconscious, but from a totally different direction. The spirit is not the unconscious mind. The unconscious is part of the *soul*. The spirit is an entirely different area, and it is through the spirit that God comes in as we have shown.

Dr. Thomas A. Harris says about the conscious and subconscious mind, "The evidence seems to indicate that everything which has been in our conscious awareness is recorded in detail and stored in the brain and is capable of being 'played back' in the present."[1] Many of the responses of the past are played back in the present when someone jabs us in a psychological sore spot.

The subconscious mind has a lot of hurtful memories stuffed into it. "Out of sight—out of mind" is not valid here. What is blocked out of our conscious memory will still influence and color our thinking and actions unless

[1]Thomas A. Harris, M.D., *I'm OK, You're OK* (New York, N.Y.: published by arrangement with Harper & Row Publishers, Inc., 1967) pages 25 and 26.

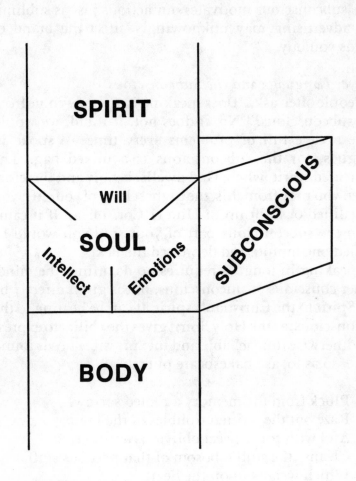

it's healed. If an emotional wound is too deep, one cannot merely use intelligence and willpower to solve the problem. Problems in the subconscious are involuntary. The subconscious motivates our actions just as subliminal advertising may unknowingly affect the brand of goods you buy.

Prayer Language and the Subconscious

People often ask, "Does speaking in tongues come from the subconscious?" No, it does not. If it did, we would have a cage full of problems every time we spoke in tongues, for the subconscious is a mixed bag. The re-created spirit, where God dwells, is holy and therefore when you pray from this, the highest level of your life, you are edified or built up in Him (1 Cor. 14:4a). If it came from the subconscious part of your soul you would be edified one minute and depressed the next.

Speaking in tongues requires no data from the mind, either conscious or unconscious, but is given directly by the Spirit to the Christian's spirit. It can be healing to the unconscious, as the Holy Spirit gives the ability to express the otherwise unreachable and inexpressible needs found there, so as to, as Shakespeare puts it:

> Pluck from the memory a rooted sorrow,
> Raze out the written troubles of the brain,
> And with some sweet oblivious antidote,
> Cleanse the stuff'd bosom of that perilous stuff
> Which weighs upon the heart.
> ("Macbeth," Act V, Scene 3)

Jamie Buckingham, prolific writer and speaker, reminds us in his book on inner healing that praying in tongues is a valuable tool for soul healing.[2] Many have found this so and have said things like, "When I began to pray in tongues it was as if my mind was a tape recorder. As I prayed God was erasing the old negative memories and then recording over them with His good words and impressions." The Basic English Translation quotes Romans 8:26a this way: "The Holy Spirit helps our infirmities with words that are not in our power to say." Infirmities can be weaknesses or ailments in soul or body. It's great to know that God can guide our prayers on a level beyond our understanding.

Even though you have this God-given ability to speak in tongues you may still need further help with specific, soul-healing prayer. Make use of every means God has made possible for your healing. God works in many ways to bring about wholeness.

Soul Healing—Inner Healing

In recent times, we have been learning a lot more of how we can work with Jesus, as He seeks to heal the parts of our souls that lie below consciousness. This is often called "Inner Healing." We most often use the term, "Healing of the Soul," or just "Soul Healing."

Paul's counsel in his letter to the Philippians is: ". . . Work out your own salvation with fear and trembling. For it is God which works in you both to will and to do of His good pleasure" (Phil. 2:12b, 13, KJV modernized).

If we've accepted Jesus, God is in us and has brought new life to our spirits. He's working *in* us. On the other hand, we must cooperate with God so His life can be worked *out* in all facets of our lives. Soul healing is one of the ways salvation is being worked out in you.

When you received Jesus as Savior He came into your

---

[2] Jamie Buckingham, *Risky Living* (Plainfield, N.J.: Logos International, 1976), page 38.

spirit—heaven came into you. Your spirit was totally healed and "justified," everything about it was made "*just right.*" It was "just-as-if-I'd" never been out of fellowship with God. Your soul and body were touched by God at the same time, and the process of restoration begun. As we've seen, though, there's a lot more resistance to God's healing on the part of our souls and bodies. They aren't instantly cured, like our spirits are. Restoration in them is progressive, as the Holy Spirit is able to get them more and more under His lordship. So we say, "Your spirit was saved, your soul was saved and is being saved (restored), and your body is being saved (healed) and will be totally saved (re-created) at the resurrection."

Shirley was healed even more deeply through soul healing prayers. God, through a word of knowledge and revelation, showed her what the scary door to the basement represented. Then she opened the door to let His love heal deep in her subconscious mind and emotions.

Jesus is knocking at the door which conceals your hurting memories and damaged emotions. When you hear Him knocking all you have to do is open the door. Wherever Jesus is invited He heals and He restores. Miracles happen.

20

Does Your Soul Need Healing?

"I thought I had a happy marriage," Carl, a handsome young businessman related. "We had three beautiful kids, a lovely home, and I was moving ahead fast in my work. Then it came out. My wife had been involved with another man for several years—"

Alice had a problem liking herself. "When I was a kid, if somebody complimented me, my mother would always say 'pretty is as pretty does'! She never affirmed to me that I was really okay. She meant to keep me from pride, but actually built in a deep set of identity problems for me."

"I could only get my father's attention when I got in trouble, and received his wrath," said Joe. "So I married women, one after another, who showed me the only kind of 'love' I knew—cruel love to feed my desire to be punished, masochism."

"I was fourteen when I got tired of brutal beatings and ran away from home," explained Joan, her soft brown eyes downcast. "Hitchhiking, I was given rides by eighteen men. Three of them raped me, and another, a pervert, molested me. I reached my destination a lot worse off than when I left.''

Can these memories and lives be healed? Do you know people like this? People who are hurting? Are you a wounded person yourself?

There's good news for you. As you open the doors to the "storage areas" where these memories are kept, Jesus can cleanse and heal them. We call this soul healing and restoration. We believe it may be an important need even after you have been reborn of the Spirit through Jesus, and baptized in the Holy Spirit because the most serious blocks to the free flow of spiritual life come from these subconscious problems.

A woman we knew had a troubled childhood, with lots of potential for hurts. Marie's growing up years were not easy. Yet, when she was released in the Holy Spirit He seemed to do a pretty complete job of healing her soul. "I wept a bucket full of tears," she said. "I guess the Lord must have used them to heal the damage, because I sure haven't had many problems since."

Her husband also had a wonderful experience in receiving the baptism in the Spirit, and many good things have happened in his life as a result. Yet, through the following years he has had many soul problems: depression and times of debilitation, and still has difficulty in keeping free in the Spirit. "I had what would seem outwardly a very secure childhood," he comments. "I was a much-loved child. Yet there were some real hurts from my formative years, and I hadn't realized how deep they actually were." The baptism in the Spirit helped to show him the needs, but didn't completely cure him. This man has been receiving soul-healing prayer and counseling and he says, "I am amazed and delighted at a new stability in my life, and a freedom that's growing."

Both husband and wife were baptized-in-the-Spirit Christians, but their degree of inner healing was different. This is good for each of us to remember when we consider the subject of soul healing. Each of us are unique individuals at different places in growth and healing.

Does Everyone Need Soul Healing?

Does everybody need Jesus to heal their souls? Certainly not everyone has dramatic problems such as those we listed at the beginning of this chapter. Similarly, not everyone, thank goodness, has a desperate need for the healing of the body. On the other hand, we can guess that everyone has *some* need for physical healing—even if it involves only a sore toe, or some other very minor ailment. But if Jesus is ready to heal all our sickness, as the Bible says, we would be foolish not to let Him do it.

Even though you may not remember some ghastly experience, chances are there are smaller things that need a healing touch. Then, too, you can't tell what effect the healing of some seemingly unimportant trauma may have. A close friend remembered that in the first grade the teacher had ridiculed him. He let Jesus heal that hurt, and then found to his amazement that he moved out into a whole new freedom in his spiritual life. That seemingly silly and incidental experience had been holding him back far more than he could have imagined.

Every encounter with Jesus Christ has some degree of inner healing: salvation, deliverance, baptism in the Spirit, baptism with water, confession of sins, Holy Communion, recommitment to Christ, physical healing, deliverance, revelation in reading Scripture, dynamic prayer experience, inspired dreams, and others. The more

147

open you are to Jesus' love, the more healing takes place.

Healing of the soul may be needed when you have been hurt or damaged in some way by another person, experience or event outside your control. The hurt may have been caused by spouse, parents, siblings, teachers, personal friends or strangers. No one is perfect, and all but God Himself give conditional love. This being true, it seems likely that everyone to some degree has needed, presently needs, or will need soul healing.

How Can I Tell if I Need Healing for My Soul?

You may need soul healing: if you are afraid to fly in an airplane or ride in a car; if you spend hours in a fantasy world; if you have a constant desire to be held, or don't want to be touched at all; if you had dyslexia or some other handicap in childhood; if you intensely dislike the opposite sex, or your own sex, or dislike yourself; if you can't forgive your father or mother; if you lack inner controls; if you desire to injure yourself or others; if you lived in a war zone, or were in combat; if you're obsessed with sexual desire, or abnormally cold sexually; if you have a lack of self-identity; if you have long periods of depression or overwhelming feelings of guilt; if you wish you had never been born; if you were treated cruelly or molested during childhood; if you can't think of anyone who loved you during the first six years of your life; if you feel God doesn't love you; if you've had someone close to you die— especially if it was a sudden or tragic death; if you were in an accident and saw someone injured or killed.

You may also need prayer: if your mother had a long and hard delivery, or you were an "instrument baby"; if you were put into an incubator for a period, or your mother was unable to care for you or even be with you at all for several days or weeks after your birth; if you were born out of wedlock, or were unwanted; or if your parents wanted you to have been the opposite sex. (Adopted children, although usually much wanted and loved, often have need of healing because of having been rejected by their natural parents—or because they feel they have been.)

If your mother died at your birth, or your father or mother died during the first few years of your life, your parents separated while you were young, you had an alcoholic parent, your father left for war, or for business, and was gone for long periods of time, or you were transplanted to a different country during your formative years, you may well need soul-healing prayer.

Further Questions That Help

Other questions which can help you include: "Who was the first person you genuinely felt loved you?" It's important to answer this honestly, not the answer you feel you *ought* to give. If you must admit, "I didn't feel loved by either my father or my mother," you know you have hurts that go back to the very beginning of your life.

Another key question: "Did you have a fantasy world in your childhood, and do you still escape into it from time to time?" If you did and do, you know that you had deep hurts from which you needed to escape, and that you are still feeling those hurts. It will help a great deal, by the way, to talk about your "secret world" with someone you know and trust; it may help a lot in further understanding and revealing problems.

Other questions: "What is the first hurtful memory you have?" "Did you like yourself when you were a child?" "Did you have a happy childhood?" "When do you first remember being happy?" "Were you told you were selfish?" (Often the "selfish" child is simply too hurt to grow up. When no one else seems to, you care for "number one" in order to survive.)

Fill in the blanks on these: "My father gave me a picture of myself as ...."

"My mother gave me a picture of myself as ....
...."

Highly crucial is: "If you could have had the choice, would you have chosen to be born at all?" If you answer "no" to this, it reveals a very deep rejection of yourself, and of life in general, and God, too, who created it all. "Would you have wanted to been born into an all-male world? An all-female world?" A "yes" to either of these could indicate a deep rejection of the opposite sex or the same sex.

The way you answer these questions will show whether there are areas in your soul Jesus still needs to be let into. These questions are not asked to lead into some kind of psychoanalysis or psychological therapy, but in order to find the needs so you can ask the Lord to heal them. Once you start, the Holy Spirit will guide you from one thing to the next in the order He selects.

When root causes are discovered, interconnected branch memories can then be discovered.

Getting Ready to Pray

The first step then is realizing your need and wanting to be healed. Two women came to talk to Rita at a meeting in

Southern California. Mary had family needs and Maxine came to support her. Rita told Mary, "The best thing you can do to help your family is get healed yourself from your own hurtful memories and experiences. As that occurs, then God will be able to open doors for you to help family members." Rita then turned to Maxine and said, "And you can help Mary pray and Mary can in turn pray for you."

Maxine looked at her with some dismay on her pretty face, and replied, "Oh, I can't pray with Mary, you see I don't pray out loud."

Rita asked, "What in your childhood could have caused you to have trouble expressing yourself?"

"I never saw any connection before," she answered thoughtfully, "but perhaps it is because I was tongue-tied as a child."

Rita asked, "What is the most hurtful scene you remember along these lines?"

Maxine recalled, "When I was six years old, my older brother and I were standing on a dock in Florida. He asked me to say, 'City dock.' I did and it came out sounding like an obscene word. He laughed and laughed. I was humiliated."

"You know, Maxine, Jesus was there with you on that dock. He is love in perfection. He hurt when you hurt." Rita went on, "Try to visualize the original scene in your mind's eye, but this time see Jesus there."

Maxine closed her eyes and responded, "Yes, I do see Him," she replied. "He's standing at the end of the dock, and I'm in the middle, wearing my yellow dress."

"What is Jesus doing at the end of the dock?" Rita asked.

"Well, He's holding His arms out to me saying, 'I want

all the little children to come to me, and I'm going to Him. Now He's holding me in His arms. My brother is joining us and Jesus is forgiving him and has His arm around him." She began to weep. After the tears subsided Rita led her in prayer, speaking forgiveness to her brother. She was healed and she knew it.

Maxine didn't have any idea she needed healing until God revealed it to her supernaturally. The list of questions we gave can help, but the Holy Spirit, through the gifts of knowledge and wisdom, can get right to the root of things very quickly. As soon as Maxine saw her need, she also wanted healing, and received it. A few months later she wrote to say she has a growing confidence in her ability to pray out loud with others.

This example shows how simple soul-healing prayer can be—simple, but at the same time, profound—as all God's things are. Maxine needed healing from being laughed at and humiliated, and she received it. Maxine and Mary said they intended to go on and pray further, now that they had grasped the principle.

The people we cited in the first of this chapter: the young businessman and his wife, the young woman who didn't like herself, the man who wanted punishment from his wife, the abused child who ran away and got into worse trouble—Carl, Alice, Joe, John, Maxine, and Shirley and thousands more like them, are having their lives and memories healed. The more we pray, the more we realize there is nothing too hard for God.

If you find the blessings of God receding in your own life, or you find yourself faced by problems that baffle you, involving your feelings and attitudes and those of others around you, or if you just plain feel you are not moving as joyfully in the Holy Spirit as you'd like to be, this may be your answer. Why don't you let Jesus heal your soul.

152

21

What You Can Do About It

After you have recognized you have a need, what do you do about it? You ask Jesus to heal your *soul*, just as you would ask Jesus to heal your *body*, and just as He healed your *spirit* when He came to live in you. In fact, one of the reasons soul healing has only recently attracted such attention in the Christian world isn't because it's new, but because we have in the past failed to distinguish between soul and spirit. We therefore didn't see that the soul might still need healing even though the spirit has been brought to new life in Christ.

We aren't talking about "poor man's psychiatry." If you pray with someone and ask Jesus to heal his soul, you aren't practicing psychiatry any more than you would be practicing medicine if you asked Jesus to heal his body. You can pray by yourself for soul healing, just as you can pray by yourself for the healing of your body, but it helps in both to have compassionate persons praying with you, letting God's healing flow through them to you.[1]

Just how do you go about it? You're probably familiar with a "plan of salvation," a logical sequence of steps based on Holy Scripture to help in leading someone to accept Jesus as Savior. We'd like to offer a "plan for soul healing," an orderly series of steps, based on Scripture, to guide you in letting Jesus heal the hurts in your life.

Step One—Share Your Hurts

Talk about the hurtful memories with trustworthy friends. The Scripture says: "Confess your faults one to another, and pray for one another, that you may be healed." Note that it says "faults," not "sins."[2] A fault is a defect or an injury, something you can't help, like a short leg. It may have come by heredity, or through an accident or mistreatment, but you didn't cause it. A *sin* on the other hand, is something you do intentionally, knowing it to be wrong. You have a choice about it.

A "fault" is like an earthquake *fault.* It is a crack in the personality that can lead to a real shake-up if it is not repaired. Faults are not sins, but they can lead to sin if they are not attended to. In general, soul healing is not a confessional, although if the person counseled feels the need of God's forgiveness, he should be guided to receive it according to his own belief and custom. (If the person you

---

[1]In soul healing, we like to have two helpers praying with each person, if possible, as this gives more opportunity for the Holy Spirit to minister His gifts. Our Lord set the pattern of "two by two" (Luke 10:1) and we've experienced the wisdom of His doing so. It's best in general for women to pray with women, and men with men. This is not an absolute rule, except it obviously wouldn't be best for a man to pray with a woman, except from his own family, without another woman present. Husbands and wives can be very effective, either praying for each other, or as a team praying with others. One of the first requirements for anyone who wants to help in this way is to keep what is said confidential. The two counselors may discuss between themselves what has been shared, but under no circumstances should it be told to anyone else without clear permission from the person prayed with.

[2]It is interesting to note that the Greek versions differ here, some using the word *paraptoma,* rather than the usual word in the New Testament for "sin," which is *hamartia.* Other translations give this as "Confess your sins one to another. . . ." But the King James translators, realizing that you don't confess your sins "one to another," nor do you pray for sin to be "healed" but *forgiven,* and seeing that *paraptoma* can be translated, "lapse, deviation, error (unintentional)," chose the word, "fault." We believe they were highly perceptive in doing this.

are praying with has no pastoral relationship with any church, and no custom concerning confession, we suggest that you direct him to your own minister or priest, or that you assist him in offering his sins to God, and then give him assurance of God's forgiveness in words such as these:

"I have heard you confess your sins to God, and I assure you by the Word of God, that He has forgiven you. Scripture says: 'If we confess our sins He is faithful and just to forgive us our sins and to cleanse us from all unrighteousness' " 1 John 1:9 KJV.)

In the healing of the soul, we are talking about healing these injuries or defects in the personality which have been caused by past experiences and relationships, especially those of childhood.

Let the Holy Spirit show you or those working with you where to begin. The list of questions in the previous chapter will be useful. When the Holy Spirit has brought an event to your mind that needs healing, visualize the scene as vividly as you can. Recall any details such as other people who were there, what you were wearing, what the place looked like and so forth. Share what you can with those praying with you.

Step Two—God Is Omnipresent

Having done this, realize *Jesus was there* with you. How do we know? Both Old and New Testaments teach that God is present everywhere, and officially Christians are supposed to believe it. Jeremiah, the prophet, says, "Can any hide himself in secret places that I shall not see him? saith the Lord. Do not I fill heaven and earth? saith the Lord" (Jer. 23:24 KJV).

"You have surrounded me behind and before, and laid your hand upon me. Such knowledge is too wonderful for me;

it is high, I cannot comprehend it. Where shall I go from your Spirit? Or where shall I flee from your presence? If I ascend up into heaven, you are there: if I make my bed in hell, you are there. If I take the wings of the morning, and dwell in the depths of the sea, even there will your hand lead me, and your right hand will hold me" (Ps. 139:5-10 KJV, modernized; see also Prov. 15:3, Acts 17:27, 28, Heb. 13:8, Ps. 139:13).

You don't have to ask Jesus to go *back* with you to the hurtful event. If the Triune God is always present, then Jesus, who is the second person of the Trinity, was with you every moment of your past life, just as He is today.[3] But you *do* need to acknowledge that He was there so He can manifest Himself to you and help you (John 14:21b). Jesus couldn't do any "mighty works" in His own home town because they didn't acknowledge who He was. Scripture says: "In *all your ways* acknowledge Him and He shall direct your paths" (Prov. 3:6 KJV, modernized).

Rita tells this story for an example: "Shortly after I was baptized in the Holy Spirit in 1960, a friend, Barbara Service, and I were asked to pray for a woman for the baptism with the Spirit. We knew nothing about her. We went to her small, but neat, home in Tampa, Florida, and met a woman who was probably in her forties.

"After witnessing to and praying for her, in a voice filled with awe and complete surprise she described a vision she was having. She said, 'Oh, I see Jesus right there in the upper corner of the room.' Then she relayed the message He gave her, 'Oh, Jesus, you've been with me all the time. Through all the trials you've been with me and I didn't even know it. Jesus, you've been with me all the time!'

---

[3]We're not trying to negate the idea of "healing of memories" in which the person asks Jesus to go back and heal the hurts of the past. On the other hand, some folks have resisted this approach because they feel they are telling the Lord what to do. We find it most helpful to remind people that "Jesus was there all the time." This is the way God has led us to teach it, and it does have good support in Scripture.

"Barbara and I were so amazed, never having had a vision ourselves or having been with a person who did. We didn't know whether to keep our eyes tightly shut, or open them, or perhaps fall on our faces!

"Finally, after many tears of joy, our friend explained to us that her husband had left her years before. She had no skills and so went to work as a housekeeper for long hours to feed and clothe her children. Now Jesus had healed the hurts of the past by revealing His presence to her through all those difficult times.

"I didn't realize it then," says Rita, "but God was showing me a very important key to healing of the soul which He would remind me of years later—His omnipresence."

To recognize that Jesus was with you through all your life is healing in itself.[4] In praying for soul healing we not only visualize Him there, but acknowledge the reality that He truly *was* there—God giving the eyes of faith to see it.

God told Moses: "My presence shall go with you . . ." (Exod. 33:14a, modernized). The Psalmist said: "You will show me the path of life; in your presence is fulness of joy; . . ." (Ps. 16:11).

Another Psalm reminds us, "Let us come before His presence with thanksgiving" (Ps. 95:2a). Another, "Enter into His gates [presence] with thanksgiving and praise" (Ps. 100:4a).

Don't compare the intensity of the awareness of God's presence in your life to another's. Sensations such as warmth, "heavenly goose flesh" (as Dr. Bill Reed calls it), tears, joy, peace, even visions, are individual responses. Those who have difficulty sensing God's presence will be healed just as surely as anyone else as they yield their wills to God.

---

[4] When we say God was there all the time, we don't mean to imply He was standing by, consenting to evil. Evil has come into the world through man's choice to disobey God. Since we've been given free will, God can only change things in our lives as we permit Him to. "And He did not many mighty works there [His own home town] because of their unbelief" (Matt. 13:58, KJV).

The Scripture teaches that God is present at all times. If we accept Jesus and the freedom of His Spirit, then as our souls are healed we will become even *more* aware of His presence.

Step Three—God Is Perfect Unconditional Love

Jesus prayed before His death, "That the love wherewith you [Father] loved me may be in them . . ." (John 17:26b). "As the Father loved me," says Jesus, "so have I loved you. Continue in my love" (John 15:9). We have the same love Jesus received from His Father now dwelling in us, because Jesus prayed for this as a final request before His death. To the same measure His Father loved Him, Jesus loves us!

"Behold, what manner of love the Father has bestowed upon us, that we should be called the sons of God . . ." (1 John 3:1a). "Hereby perceive we the love of God, because He laid down His life for us . . ." (1 John 3:16a). What honor and joy to be received by God as His children, His own family, His offspring. The greatest love is seen when Jesus—perfect man—willingly laid down His own life to rescue us from eternal death.

"Jesus did not come to steal, kill, or destroy, rather He came to give us *life* more abundantly" (John 10:10, paraphrase by authors). Anything that smacks of death and destruction comes from the enemy, Satan. Life, health and wholeness come from our loving God.

Often after teaching on soul-healing prayer, people will say things like: "I have never been able to recognize and accept my Father God's love before, but I can today." "For the first time I feel that God is good and He loves me." God says to Jeremiah and also to us: "I have loved you with an everlasting love: therefore with lovingkindness have I drawn you" (Jer. 31:3b, KJV, modernized).

The best story in which to see the Father's love for us is in the Parable of the Prodigal Son (Luke 15:11-24). Notice the father's unconditional love. He didn't hold back love; he gave all freely. This is the love God wants you to experience as He heals all the crippling memories of the past and walks on with you into the future.

First Corinthians 13 is that great chapter of love. Read verses four through eight, substituting "God" (Father, Son and Holy Spirit) in the place of "charity" or "love." Realize God has and is all these attributes and more. "God is love" (1 John 4:8).

God is love and God is good. So often Christians sound like they think He is out to make them suffer and to take all enjoyment away. They're not sure God would be concerned about them or their problems.

God is more loving than the greatest earthly parent who ever existed. He's not out to condemn us but to make us happy and fulfilled in every way (Luke 11:11-13).

Meditate upon how much Jesus loves you. Sense that love. Know He is with you right now. When you feel secure in Jesus' loving presence, you are ready to pray about any situation.

Step Four—By Faith, See Jesus, and What He Does

By faith, then, see Jesus in the scene. He may be in everyday clothes, or in biblical dress. You may just see a silhouette, or only see His eyes or His hands. Some can't visualize Him at all, but they can feel His presence, or see a light and know it's coming from Him.

Now go through that hurtful experience again. How different it is now that you know Jesus is there, supporting you with His love! Tell Him how you feel, how you hurt inside. He will be to you what you need most.

As you see Jesus in the past situation, let other things begin to come into focus: how much Jesus loves you—and the others, the reason for the behavior of the people who hurt you, and the good points of those people. See how incidents build on one another to cause deeper hurts, and pray for one thing after another as the Spirit leads.

Tell those praying with you what you see. You are actively participating and cooperating in the healing. The Holy Spirit will give you insight and show you what Jesus is doing. He may also show the people praying with you things that will greatly help you.

Just before the Passover, some Greeks who came to worship at the feast said to the disciple Philip: "Sir, we would see Jesus" (John 12:21). He was the only one they wanted to see; no one else would do. At that time they could see Jesus physically; but now we see Him by faith (2 Cor. 5:16 KJV).

So a main theme in soul-healing prayer is: "We would see Jesus." As we see Jesus in every situation healing comes. No matter what hurt we received, when we see Jesus there, it no longer hurts as it once did. We can go into any situation, from any time frame, knowing Jesus is there with us. The well-known song says: "Turn your eyes upon Jesus, look full in His wonderful face; and the things of earth will grow strangely dim in the light of His glory and grace."[5]

After His resurrection, Jesus walked to Emmaus with a downcast pair of disciples, who did not recognize who He was. He drew them out so they would share their troubles with Him. Jesus cheered them up when He explained the Scriptures to them, and showed them, all the way from Genesis to Malachi, how it told the Messiah was going to

---

[5]Words and Music by H.H. Lemmel, 1922, assigned to Singspiration, Inc.; All rights reserved. By kind permission.

"suffer and enter into His glory" and He proceeded to show them all the way through "the things concerning Himself." When they had read or heard Scriptures before, Jesus had been there in the Book, but they had not seen Him. Now as He "opened the Scriptures" to them, their "hearts burned within them" as they saw Jesus throughout (Luke 24:13-45).[6]

We were talking about this story in a class for counselors, when the Lord gave one of them, Helen Lucas, this insight: "That's the way it is with our old lives," she said. "They're like the Old Testament. We can't see Jesus in them, yet He was there all the time! Now we are letting Jesus Himself show us that He was there, and as we see Him and let Him speak to us, we are healed." Once again the old becomes new.

It's as if God were making a new "movie" of the original scene. The events are basically the same but the "plot" is different. God doesn't change the actual history but He changes the history of the heart. He changes your feelings about the memory of that event. Research has shown that we record in our unconscious storage not just what actually happened, but how we *felt* about what happened, and how we interpreted it. It is this that Jesus alters and heals. The old memory loses its power to harm us. Your emotions are changed and your memory transformed by the resurrected Lord. Scripture says to "overcome evil with good" (Rom. 12:21), and that's what the Lord does in soul healing.

A friend, Janet Biggart, describes soul healing this way: "When we see the past and ask God to heal it, it's like two different pictures: the old hurtful one is in the fallen world where God isn't seen or acknowledged; in the new healed one we see Jesus and the world as He would like it to be—His world restored."

---

[6]Jesus was also known through the breaking of bread at dinner. The Lord's Supper (Mass or Holy Communion) is a wonderful follow-up to soul-healing prayer. Through it, too, our eyes should be opened to see Jesus more clearly.

So with the Greeks we say, "Sir, we would see Jesus!" Better yet, "Sir, we *will* see Jesus."

Step Five—Hear What Jesus Speaks to You and Others in the Scene

Soul-healing prayer is an exercise in knowing what God is saying to you. (This usually refers to an inner knowing, deep inside, rather than an audible voice.) We read the Scripture, "My sheep hear my voice, and I know them, and they follow me" (John 10:27), but we often find it hard to believe that we can know or hear our Lord's voice. Again Jesus says, "Everyone who is of the *truth* hears my voice" (John 18:37b, KJV modernized).

It seems strange that God's people in the Old Testament heard so clearly and easily from God whereas we hardly expect to today. They had God with them, but not God joined to them permanently, as we have through Jesus and the Holy Spirit. Yet they heard from God and we so rarely expect to.

Some people say since we have Scripture, we don't need to hear from God in any other way. Scripture is our guide to evaluate what we hear, to tell whether it is indeed from God, yet God doesn't always quote Scripture every time He speaks to us. Sometimes Jesus does speak directly from Scripture in soul-healing prayer. Other times it's a direct personal word. What God says, of course, will never contradict the Scriptures.

Because we have been trying to forgive everyone and keep our eyes on Jesus, we are more open and receptive to hear from our Lord. We expect Him to guide and direct our thoughts, ideas, what we see and hear. We're ready to receive His words with childlike faith.

Just as presumed vocal gifts of the Spirit such as prophecy

are to be checked and evaluated by the hearers, so it is in this. Openness to hear from the Lord grows with experience. That's why it's good to have several praying together for check and balance. Just as ministry in prophecy, interpretation, or knowledge may be 70 percent the Holy Spirit and 30 percent the person's own ideas, so it may be here. The words may not be 100 percent accurate, but the general theme will be, and God will use it.

Hearing from God gives us new perspective. We are no longer limited by our own subjective view of things. We can begin to see situations from Jesus' viewpoint. When we see through Jesus' eyes our vision improves immeasurably!

Step Six—Speak What You See and Hear

When you prayed to receive the baptism in the Holy Spirit, you trusted God, opened your mouth and began to speak in faith, and your prayer language was there. In the same way, if you have brought prophecy, you know it's a matter of being willing to speak out whatever the Holy Spirit is giving you.

Speaking out by faith what you see Jesus doing and hear Him saying is similar. It may be a little difficult at first, but you will gain confidence as you experience confirmation and healing. As in prophecy, it is speaking forth as you are guided by the Holy Spirit.

The spoken word has power. Scripture says, "With the mouth confession is made unto salvation." Speaking forth what God shows you impresses it more deeply on your soul. Others too can rejoice as they are let in on the special things God is doing inside you.

Step Seven—Forgive and Speak Forgiveness

Jesus said, "And when you stand praying, forgive, if you

have ought against any: that your Father also who is in heaven may forgive you your trespasses" (Mark 11:25, KJV modernized). God does not here say, "Ask forgiveness for what you've done wrong"; He's telling you, "Forgive others for what they've done to you."

If you don't forgive other people, God can't release you from the effect of your own sins. This is a basic principle. If you want to be able to receive love, you must be willing to love; if you want to receive forgiveness, you must forgive.

God has told us to forgive those who have harmed us, and if we're trying to obey Him, we decide: "Okay, I'll forgive them!" But we know how hard it is, because if we forgive, we may not be on guard and will leave ourselves open to be hurt again. So our attempted forgiveness often ends with "*Watch* it next time!" Any family member knows this kind of forgiveness: we forgive until the person offends us again, and then we bring up all the past things he or she has done. We didn't really forgive—we just declared a truce!

If the person being prayed with hasn't even attempted to forgive at this level, if they are consciously holding resentment against people who have wronged them, the whole process will be blocked. You will need to begin by having them forgive, or even tell God that they *want* to forgive, though they may not feel like it.

Forgiving at the Deepest Level

When Jesus heals our memories through soul-healing prayer, He makes it possible for us to forgive in a new way. The original hurt is made as though it had never been, and since we no longer feel the hurt, we are not fearful of being hurt again. We are not afraid to forgive and love the person who wronged us. We are free to see him or her through God's eyes, and with God's compassion.

When you are able to forgive someone freely and fully, because Jesus has healed you, you yourself are released from any bondage to that person. Whenever you are holding a grudge, you leave yourself open to attack from the enemy, and deprive yourself of God's protection at that point. Conversely, when you truly forgive, you free yourself from attack, and you are able to receive God's protection and love in the area of need.

Forgiving at the level of the emotions and subconscious is the climax of your healing. It goes beyond initial mental assent which is basic and also important. It's easier to forgive at this deepest level *after* we're healed because we're then so filled with the love of Jesus. This level of forgiveness is not "necessary to salvation," but it *is* necessary if you want to live as happily and effectively as possible.

Before praying we often say something like, "I know you, being a sincere Christian, have tried to forgive everyone, but now we want you to do it in a little different way, this time from the vantage point of where the original hurt, and now the healing, has occurred." We also find it helpful to say to the person, "Remember when we encourage you to forgive, we are not condoning the other person's sin against you. We don't like what they did either, but we are helping you follow Jesus' example for living." Forgiving doesn't mean you have to accept another's ethics, or morality, or even make them your closest friend. But it does mean you will love them because genuine forgiveness always manifests itself in love.

When you are ready to speak forgiveness, see yourself at the age you were when the incident happened, and speak from that age as much as you can. If you were eight years old when you were hurt, for example, forgive the persons involved as from your eight-year-old self. What you're really doing is giving Jesus a way to extend His infinite forgiveness into the emotions of your past. Either way, past or present, God is eager to minister to anyone who is obeying Him by forgiving.

Here again, confess it with your lips. Speak in the first person, present tense, to get as close to the original scene as you can. This seems to bring greater release. Jesus in Scripture doesn't give us many details on how to forgive. He just says, "Do it," then He gives us all the assistance possible to help us obey Him.

So at the end of each session you guide the one being prayed with to speak forgiveness to each person involved. He or she is speaking to them as in the past event, in that time and place. All times and places are present to Jesus, so you can say: "Jack, or Jane, through Jesus, I forgive you for hurting me. I set you free and will not hold this against you any longer. I am healed and will not be hurt by this memory any more. Jesus has set me free."[7]

Here's a check list of people to make sure you've forgiven. You may need to forgive your spouse, children, parents (or others in that role), grandparents and great-grand-parents, other authority figures, brothers, sisters, cousins, neighbors, teachers, ministers, military officers, law officers, institutions, etc.—not forgetting *yourself*.

How about forgiving God? Some people are angry with God, though He has done nothing to deserve anger. One woman forgave God for loving so much that He gave humanity free will, through which sin and sickness could

---

[7]Scientists who study the mind say all that's ever happened to us is recorded in memory, including the way we felt about it. In soul-healing, the Holy Spirit goes back through the recording to those experiences. He changes feelings, and removes scars as we relive the scenes with Jesus.

Please note that we are not here proposing some kind of telepathy, or communication with the departed (in the case that a person or persons in the past event are no longer in this life). The forgiveness is offered as in the past and to the people who were there at that time. This can happen through Jesus, for all times are present to Him.

come into the world. And that's God's only "mistake," if you will, loving us too much. Yet the anger needs to be admitted, as often we find it is anger at our own earthly father misdirected.

Don's Story

Take Don, for example. When he first found out about the power of Jesus through the Holy Spirit, he was in serious shape psychologically. Doctors had treated him in various ways, but found no solution. Don was told about the power of the Holy Spirit by a college professor, who became aware of Don's difficulties. Through this deeply committed man, Don received the baptism in the Holy Spirit and his life was wonderfully changed.

For fifteen years he has been a consistent witness for Jesus in his church, an example to everyone of what God can do. Don's pastor says, "If you were to ask me for an example in my congregation of someone with very few problems, who was consistently happy and free in the Spirit, and a highly effective person, I would point out Don."

Recently, however, Don admitted that although his life had been dramatically changed by receiving the power of the Spirit, he still was aware of fears and depression that kept him from having the freedom he knew he should enjoy.

He began to pray and counsel with two friends from the church. In fact, what happened to Don was one of the "eye-openers" that made us realize how important soul healing is.

Don was a highly satisfactory person to work with because after his weekly prayer-counseling session he let God continue healing him all week long. When he came back for prayer he always had exciting things to share about what the Lord had done and shown him that week.

We'll choose a typical prayer session as an example. Counselor 1 asked Don if he had forgiven his mother for her negative, nagging attitude when he was growing up.

He answered, "Oh, numerous times."

The counselor said, "Sometimes we have to forgive the same person many times, for many different situations where we recall being hurt. Remember the seventy times seven principle in Scripture? It doesn't just mean forgiving four hundred and ninety different people. It may mean forgiving *one* person four hundred and ninety times, which always seems harder!"

Don agreed, "Right on!"

When asked if he'd remembered any particular hurtful event that occurred during his childhood, Don told about an argument over a bicycle. "Being the oldest child," Don explained, "I got a bike first. In time I outgrew it. But no one seemed to notice. I eventually took matters into my own hands and talked my parents into getting me a new one. I said my little sister could have the one I'd outgrown. She was thrilled, but after about two months she began to complain because *she* hadn't been given the new one!"

Instead of Don's mother correcting his sister and telling her to be satisfied and wait her turn to get a new bike, Don remembered his mother supported his sister, and nagged and nagged him about his "unfairness."

As they prayed about the scene, Don saw his red and black bike. He was on one side of it and his family on the other. It was hard for him to picture Jesus there at all. Said counselor 2, "In all thy ways acknowledge Him and He will direct thy paths! Don, you need to acknowledge Jesus in this scene. God is present everywhere and He was there whether you see Him or not."

Suddenly Don said, "Yeah, I see Him and He's mad at me! *He* says I'm wrong too! I think He's like all the rest of the adults. He's on their side! It makes me angry!"

Counselor 2 was a bit shaken by Don's being angry with the Lord, and began to protest, but counselor 1 spoke up, "No, I believe it's okay for Don to see it this way and to feel how angry and unhappy he is about it. This is how all adults appear to you, Don, including the Lord—unfair and uncaring.

"But now let's see Jesus as He really is, perfect love and perfect fairness. Let's pray: Lord, we bring Don and his anger to you. Draw out all this anger and fill him with your unconditional love. And if there's any spirit of anger here, I bind you in Jesus' name and command you to depart. Jesus, fill Don's soul with your love and peace."

Don smiled, "I see Jesus in a blue robe and He's put His arms around me and is comforting me. He's just holding and loving me and telling me everything is okay. He's helping me to reach out to forgive all adults for their unfairness. He brings to mind other authority figures I need to forgive: the police, some teachers—especially some physical education instructors. I didn't realize I had a problem with authority before."

"Oh, yes, I'm forgiving my sister too and giving her a hug. She hasn't been loved enough either." Then counselor 2 led Don to speak forgiveness to each person, trying to do so as much as possible from the standpoint of himself as a child, at the age when the hurt occurred.

During twelve sessions many things were dealt with and there was more healing and more forgiveness. Now Don has a line of people at his door he's helping. The healing is being passed on. This, by the way, is one of the beautiful things about soul healing.

Summary

Have you heard people say, "The past is past; there is nothing you can do about it"? We disagree. God is not just able to heal the present moments, but the past too.

All things stored in your brain are capable of being played back in the present; God can play them back through prayer—this time with us *knowing* He is with us.

We're not advocating living in the past. We believe in living in the *now* with hope for the future. What we've found to be true though, is if our pasts aren't healed we *will* live in the past rather than the present! As you allow Jesus to heal your past hurts, so you will more and more realize that He is with you in every present situation and can heal you immediately, keeping you free to love and enjoy Him, and to love and enjoy other people too. Thus soul healing becomes a daily walk with Jesus, what Brother Lawrence called "Practicing the Presence of God."

If you walk daily practicing Jesus' presence, you may receive healing when needed right then and there. This should be our goal. You can practice the healing presence of Jesus in the present as well as the past. Soul healing then is an ongoing process.

Dr. Robert Frost says, "The Lord wants not only to forgive our past, but to heal it as well! Furthermore, the past is also to be redeemed for God's glorious purpose in our lives for the future. Past mistakes, failures and even tragedies are a part of the 'all things' which God promised He would work together for our good if we continue to love Him and are committed to His ongoing purpose for our lives."[8] True fruit of soul healing is when I can look back on hard things in my life and have a thankful heart because I see how God can and has turned them to good (Rom. 8:28).

[8]Dr. Robert Frost, *Set My Spirit Free* (Plainfield, N.J., Logos International), page 116.

Further purposes for soul healing are these: to heal the body of Christ on earth so the fruit and gifts of the Spirit may flow through our lives unimpeded to heal the world. It's to have our relationship restored to God and man. It's to be about the work God has called us to and from which we have so often been sidetracked. It's to be so healed that we can get our eyes off ourselves and effectively be about our Father's business.

22

What About Deliverance?

Where does *deliverance* come into the picture? Can a person who has accepted Jesus and been born again of the Holy Spirit still have wrong spirits living in him or her that need to be cast out? Some say, "No, it's impossible. How can God and Satan occupy the same place?" Yet if you consistently pray for people in need, you know Christians do sometimes give evidence of having let in demonic forces, and do respond to deliverance prayer.

The study of the "trinity of man" explains what have seemed to be contradictory viewpoints. No, a Christian cannot have a demon in his *spirit,* but if he is foolish enough to let satanic powers in, he can give demonic spirits temporary access into his *soul.* Only an unbeliever could have the enemy indwelling spirit, soul and body, which would be true *possession.* (See the case of the Gadarene demoniac in Mark 5:1-20.)

When Christians need deliverance we realize the problem is only in the soul and/or body and that Jesus is still in the renewed spirit. Depending on the nature of the problem, we would call it oppression, obsession, depression or temporary possession of the soul. The only ground that the enemy can claim in a Christian is that which is unwisely given him.

Some who have ministries of soul healing say it should be tried before deliverance. Others say deliverance— "reclaiming from Satan your inheritance"—should regularly precede soul healing. Jesus in His earthly ministry seemed to deal with the situation as He found it. We too pray for soul healing and deliverance interchangeably, as the Holy Spirit directs.[1] We showed an example of this as we shared Don's story with you.

Sometimes Jesus cast out spirits first, sometimes He healed first. In Matthew 10:8, he told His followers, "Heal the sick, cleanse the lepers, raise the dead, cast out devils. . . ." In Luke 9:1 it reads, "And gave them power and authority over all devils, and to cure diseases." In Matthew 8:16 Jesus "cast out the spirits with His word, and healed all that were sick," but often we find Him healing the sick with no direct reference to deliverance.

The two things are interwoven. If a person has a hurt in the soul needing healing, and they have allowed that hurt to affect their behavior, it is very likely that a wrong spirit has managed to aggravate the situation. For example, take a person who has such a violent temper that he loses control of himself. It is almost certain that the temper has its root in some weakness in the soul caused by hurts from the past.

The person is not responsible for having a defect in his or her nature, but that does not make it less harmful, any more than a hereditary disease is less harmful to the person because it is hereditary, and not caused by his own bad living habits. If, however, the person gives way

---

[1]A handy mini-book on the subjects of inner healing and deliverance is: Father Francis MacNutt, *Healing Through Prayer* (New York: Bantam Books, 1977).

again and again to the temper, allowing it to rule him, it is very likely that a spirit of anger will invade the soul, and will need to be cast out. Whenever you find a situation that the person says is uncontrollable, or compulsive, you can expect a need for deliverance.

How to Pray

How do you deal with it? Well, it's best if *you* don't! Instead, lead the person to do it for himself or herself, while you back them up and agree. It's very simple. Claiming the protection and the power of the blood of Jesus, have them name the thing that's troubling them, bind it and order it to depart in the name of Jesus. For example, if the problem seems to be uncontrollable anger, the person should say something like this: "Spirit of anger, I bind you, and cast you out in the name of Jesus, under His precious blood. Amen." Wrong spirits may often be named by the results they produce. Following this, the counselor should lay hands on the person's head and ask, "Lord, please fill your son (or daughter) with your Holy Spirit in every area of his (or her) life.[2]

Dr. Bob Ervin and his wife, Lucy, a lay couple who minister together, found this Scripture they like, since it refers to deliverance and soul healing combined: "Lord God, other lords beside you have had dominion over us: but we will make mention of thy name. They are dead (demons cast out are as dead to us, no more in control), they shall not live; (their works are stopped) they are destroyed, and have made all their memory to perish (healing of memories where demonic spirits have been let in)" (Isa. 26:13, 14, paraphrased by authors). This Scripture shows healing of the soul can take place

[2]Before you begin to pray with someone for deliverance, be sure they understand their threefold nature.

through deliverance prayers, when such prayers are handled properly.

Deliverance Isn't Enough

There's been a lot said and done about deliverance in recent times. Some have rather majored in it, teaching that most of the problems of human life can be solved by casting out wrong spirits. Yet it certainly does seem to help, no question about that. Says Dennis: "A young fellow came to my office one day. 'I'm just full of fear,' he said, 'and I don't know why.'

" 'Do you remember anything in your life, especially in your childhood, that would account for your fearfulness?' I inquired. 'For example, you might have been attacked by a dog when you were very little. You might not even remember it.'

"The young man started to laugh. 'That's funny,' he said. 'I *was* bitten by a dog when I was only eighteen months old. I don't remember it at all, but my parents told me about it.'

"We prayed, and cast out the spirit of fear that had come into this man's life through that early event which he couldn't even remember. The fear that had been infiltrating his life disappeared, and he 'went on his way rejoicing.' "

Beautiful! But there's just one thing wrong with it. So often the spirits that have been cast out come back again. People don't always stay free. Why not?

It's really quite simple. If you pray for deliverance, but don't go on to help the person get healed in his or her soul, you are treating the symptoms, but not getting to the root cause. The enemy spirits are able to do their dirty work because they can hide in those areas of the soul that have been closed to God because of hurts. Deliverance prayers combined with soul healing will last. "The truth sets you free" and *keeps* you free.

So deliverance prayers work in cooperation with soul healing. With the understanding of the triune person explained first, the person won't be frightened by deliverance prayers. He will know he's not possessed by wrong spirits, but God is living in him to empower him to cast away evil (James 4:7). Deliverance often takes place spontaneously during soul-healing prayer. As the person receives more and more healing in the soul from Jesus, deliverance prayers are less and less needed.

Resisting the Enemy

The extreme teaching on deliverance encouraged people to think that their troubles could all be cured by casting out wrong spirits. "You have problems with laziness? Cast out the spirit of laziness and you'll be okay! You won't have to discipline yourself to get up on time in the morning, because once that wrong spirit is gone, you'll just find yourself springing up eagerly to greet the new day!" As the old saying goes, "The devil made me do it," and if I can just get rid of him, I'll be perfect—it isn't me that's the problem.

A pastor friend of ours tells of a good old "hillbilly" evangelist who got onto this simplified method. A woman came to him complaining of "nervousness." "Praise the Lord!", he shouted, as he laid hands on her, "I cast every nerve out of your body!"

But we'd better be careful how we laugh at our friend, because we could make the same mistake about soul healing. "I don't need to make any special effort, all my problems have been taken care of by 'inner healing.' "

Nope. That's a dangerous mistake. The enemy is always pressing in to upset our apple carts, and he'll always be doing it as long as we are living in this darkened world. After deliverance, after soul healing, we still need to continue to *resist* the enemy. As we are healed it becomes much easier to do so.

Second Corinthians 10:4, 5 teaches the Christian principle of resisting attacks of the enemy on our minds and souls. Every Christian should be aware of how to do this. Here's what it says in the Phillips translation: "The very weapons we use are not those of human warfare but powerful in God's warfare for the destruction of the enemy's strongholds. Our battle is to bring down every deceptive fantasy and every imposing defense that men erect against the true knowledge of God. We even fight to capture every thought until it acknowledges the authority of Christ."

23

The Importance of the Body

We've spent a lot of time talking about the soul, because this is the part of us with most problems, and where the enemy gets in his hardest "licks." But now let's take a look at ways in which the *body* influences the outflow of the Spirit.

Your body isn't something inferior. God made it. He loves it, and He's going to glorify it, as He glorified the body of Jesus. We can't even begin to imagine what our bodies are going to look like after Resurrection Day. It says in 1 John 3:2, "It doesn't yet appear what we shall be, but we know that when He shall appear, we shall be like Him."

Your body is the final link between God's Spirit living in you and the world around you. Even if you get your soul all straightened out, so there is nothing to impede the Spirit there, and yet don't allow Him to move in and through your body, you can still keep God's love and power from reaching the world through you. This is why Satan has taught, "You must keep quiet. Don't let anyone see the joy you're feeling inside. Don't express yourself. It wouldn't be nice!" The enemy knows that even though all kinds of good things may be going on in your soul and spirit, it won't interfere with his dirty work in the world if they aren't expressed through your body.

The Value of Expression

Computer people talk about the way the intricate activities of the various integrated circuits and "chips" making up a computer are connected with the "outside world."

It's just the same with the intricate and wonderful things that go on inside you. The body is the "output circuit." If there is no connection between the inner workings of the computer and the "outside world"—no read-out of any kind—the data will be there and will have been processed, but it won't do anybody outside any good.

Or to change the figure, it's like the wheels on a car. The engine may be in great shape, the clutch and transmission in fine working order, and the differential perking along, but if there are no wheels, or if the wheels are jacked up so they don't touch the ground, the car doesn't move.

Having a body is part of being human, that's why the resurrection is so important. If you know Jesus as your Savior, then when you die (unless you are still on earth when Jesus comes on Resurrection Day) your body will be left behind, while your soul and spirit go to the Lord. But you won't really be complete until your body is raised and glorified and given back to you.

Right now, if you want God's Spirit to fill you and overflow, you've got to be willing to respond with your body as well as with your spirit and soul. This is why in "Spirit-filled" worship people need to be singing and speaking, and sometimes (in the right place and time) clapping and dancing. When Paul says that everything should be "decent and in order" he doesn't necessarily mean it should always be quiet and reserved. He means it should be in keeping with circumstances.

David du Plessis explains what this means when he points out that a man behaves differently when he is playing with his children than he does when company comes to the house. There is a time and a place. No Christian should ever behave in such a way that he or she will be thought crazy. Nor should anyone be put off or frightened by our behavior—that's a requirement of love and courtesy. On the other hand, we should be willing to express ourselves when the occasion permits. The Holy Spirit wants to inspire our whole being—spirit, soul, and body.

Things That Interfere

What can get in the way? Well, there are some obvious things, aren't there? If you take narcotics or stimulants into your body that interfere with proper function, you are impeding the Holy Spirit. A person who is drunk, or stupefied by some narcotic isn't going to be a very effective channel.

Alcohol is a problem to many, and yet the Bible does not forbid the use of alcohol, rather it forbids the *mis*use of it. For you or me, other things may be bigger problems. You may never be inclined to experiment with "mind-expanding" drugs as such, and yet be "hooked" on coffee! For us, Dennis and Rita, caffeine is a problem. We both love coffee and tea, but we can't drink them, not much anyway. If we do, it certainly interferes with our "output circuits," causing upset digestion, nervousness, and sometimes depression. What is it that can interfere with *your* physical effectiveness?

This raises another point: the soul has an influence on the body, and the body on the soul. We said previously that, although for the sake of study, we distinguish between spirit, soul, and body, that doesn't mean a human being is divided up into three independent sections but is all one person. Yet what goes on in any one of the parts will affect the other parts. The medical profession is more and more recognizing the importance of "psychosomatic" (soul-body) medicine. Some doctors claim that a very high percentage of the ills of the body are really caused by wrong attitudes in the mind (soul). And the opposite effect is also recognized, that conditions of the body can cause problems for the soul. It is increasingly evident, for example, that too much refined white sugar may cause things like depression, sleeplessness, and general psychological upset.

Seeming psychological (soul) symptoms are responding to chemical treatment of the body. An example would be giving lithium for certain emotional problems. The reason for this is that the body and soul share a common instrument in the physical brain. The brain is both a very powerful computer for data-processing and decision making, and also an elaborate control center for the body, sustained in operation by bodily functions.

How well you take care of your body with nutrition and exercise has a very definite bearing on how well the Holy Spirit can use you. At least one large Christian university in the USA (Oral Roberts University) requires students to have a regular program of exercise, as the leaders feel the school is to nurture spirit, soul, and body. This strikes us as being very wise indeed.

There is a more subtle way in which the body can be interfered with, and that is through asceticism. Asceticism is the teaching that the body is evil and must be dealt with severely: scourgings, extreme fastings, hair shirts, sleeping on hard boards, lack of proper cleanliness. All of these have been seen as forms of "holiness," and still are in some quarters. There is nothing scriptural about such things.

The Bible is not an ascetic book. There are isolated cases that seem like it. John the Baptist, or Ezekiel perhaps, but the general tenor of the Scripture is that God desires us to receive blessings for the body as well as for the spirit and soul. The Lord Himself was so far from being an "ascetic" that He was accused of gluttony and love of wine (Luke 7:34). It was an unjust accusation, of course, but it could never have been made at all if Jesus had been a gaunt ascetic, and did not take normal pleasure in eating and drinking.

Like other false teachings, this concept of mistreating the body seems to have found its way into Christianity from Eastern philosophies. It has certainly worked to the great advantage of the devil in keeping the joy and power and love of God from being shown in His people.

Some may say, "Oh, well, we don't have to worry about that. That's only those old saints and hermits in the Middle Ages! We're living in enlightened times." Wait a minute. Take a look at good "Protestant" literature—at the things which are held up as ideals of spirituality. How often is there a glorification of sickness and bodily weakness? How often is it pointed out that bodily sickness (which Jesus always healed when He was on earth) leads to great heights of spirituality? It's the same thing, the idea that the body must be humiliated and tormented in order to let the soul and spirit develop. It's even worse in the Protestant tradition because at least the medieval mystic knew that he or she was causing his or her own tortures. Often the Protestant blames them on God!

Only as the Spirit of God can truly penetrate our physical selves can He bring the kind of health and strength He wants us to have. One of Satan's last resorts to stop God's love and power from coming through His people can be to make them ill, or cause them to have accidents that will put them out of action for a while. And this can be an easy assignment for the enemy because it often goes unresisted.

Sickness certainly can bring opportunity for a person to think more seriously about life, and about God. It can be a time of great spiritual growth, but it is not God's chosen way, because for one thing it is highly inefficient! Why would God want the outflow of the Spirit interfered with even by so much as a headache or a sore throat?

There Is a Time

Yes, there are times to abstain from satisfying the desires of the body. Jesus, Himself, fasted forty days and nights. Paul said he kept his body under, and in subjection—that's fine. God is not glorified when His people are overweight. There is a time to fast. There is a time to abstain from marital relations. There is a time to endure hunger and cold, nakedness, or to put up with lack of sleep, but these are emergency situations, war-time conditions; they are not what God normally wants our bodies to experience. Paul says, "I think that in view of the impending distress it is well for a person to remain as he is . . . let those who have wives live as though they had none . . ."; but in the very same letter, just a few paragraphs before (1 Cor. 7:5) he says, "Do not refuse one another . . .", referring to marital relations.

In general, our bodies should be like clear windows that

let the light in and out, but the more effectively they work, the less we are aware of them. As a respected friend of ours, Bertha Madden, of Tampa, Florida, puts it in a charming poem:

> If I were a window
> I'd rather folks would say
> Not what a lovely window
> But what a lovely day.

The less we are aware of our bodies, the better, because then our attention can fully be given to what we do through them, or what they bring us from the world outside.

The Last Enemy

Satan's ultimate weapon to frustrate and delay God's work in the world through His people is death itself. Sixteen years ago, the baptism in the Holy Spirit was not as widely accepted in the historic churches as it is today. One of the bishops in our own branch of the church became very interested, and was strongly suggesting to his fellow bishops that they should listen to what was being taught. He had arranged for Dennis to talk with bishops about the renewal taking place at St. Luke's. He had collected a large number of written testimonies from people who had received the power of the Holy Spirit, and was working strongly in every way to get an intelligent hearing for what he perceived to be a very important matter.

Then he died. When he died, the whole plan he had been developing went to pieces. Although there is a great deal of openness to the baptism in the Holy Spirit in our denomination, if this man had lived to continue his work, we believe renewal would be much farther ahead today. Why did he die?

"Oh," you would hear someone say, "God took him. I wonder why. Perhaps God needed him more than we do!" God didn't "take" him! Satan used his strongest weapon against that person, and succeeded in removing him from the scene, and interrupting his work prematurely. God doesn't fight against Himself. No, there is real war on. It wasn't God that caused that man to die, and thus delay vital truth from being spread among God's people.

Death is an enemy. Paul says that "the last enemy that shall be destroyed is death" (1 Cor. 15:26). But if and when the enemy succeeds in causing a believer's body to die, God takes that person *out of death*! "Death is swallowed up in victory" (1 Cor. 15:54). Then God immediately proceeds to "Plan B," so that His work in the world can continue.

A Deeper Impression

No, Satan doesn't want us to express our love for God and our excitement about Him outwardly. He knows that what we express outwardly through our bodies takes a deeper hold on us inwardly. Psychologists recognize this as the old "James-Lange" principle: "Do I run because I am afraid, or am I afraid because I run?" If you are angry with someone, your anger will increase as you express it in word or action.

When you were a kid, did you ever get scared coming down the stairs in the dark, thinking there might be "something" behind you? What if you started to run? Boy, then you'd really be scared! So, on the positive side, our love for God and faith in God increases as we actively express it in word and action—with our bodies as well as our souls and spirits.

Showing Affection

Satan has managed to affix another lie onto God's people in the idea that silent contemplation of God is somehow "higher" than spoken praise. There is certainly a time for silent contemplation in the soul, but ultimately it must issue forth from the body in words of praise.

Can you imagine a guy out with his best girl who spent the entire evening *contemplating* her? Wouldn't she expect him to *say* something sooner or later? The fullness of our love and praise is not complete as long as it is just something going on *inside* us. We are three-part beings, and our whole instrument must respond.

Not only does the inhibition of our bodies keep us from expressing love to God, it also keeps us from expressing love to our fellow human beings. The bumper sticker, "Have you hugged your kid today," shows that the world is becoming aware of the principle. When you hug your children, your love for them increases, and the enemy certainly doesn't want *that*. So we have been taught not to express our affection physically, except in response to sexual drives, normal or abnormal.

Many parents are restrained from expressing physical affection to their own kids because they are afraid there might be something "wrong" with it, that there might be something incestuous about it. That's because this sad culture of ours so completely identifies physical hugging or kissing with sex—and sex alone. For the same reason, men friends tend to avoid physical contact, lest they should be thought to be homosexual.

The Holy Spirit wants to show us how to express our

affection and love to our friends and family in healthy physical actions. Many churches today are trying so hard to get people to greet one another during the service, to shake hands, to hug. The resistance to it shows the inhibitions of our culture.

Paul exhorts his friends in Corinth to "greet one another with a holy kiss."[1] (This, needless to say, does not refer to a kiss on the lips, but to a warm embrace, probably with a kiss on the cheek, that is still the normal greeting between friends in many cultures today.) J.B. Phillips, on the other hand, shows his Anglo-Saxon inhibition. He translates this, "I should like you to shake hands all round as a sign of Christian love"![2]

However, when people in the congregation have received the baptism and release of the Holy Spirit, the expression is spontaneous and joyful. They *immediately* find they have little difficulty in expressing physical affection, because the Holy Spirit has set them free to do so.

Expression of Love to the World

The actions of the Spirit through the body do not end with the expressions of affection, or even with words and actions of praise to God. Jesus said, "If you only greet your brothers, what's unusual about that?" (Matt. 5:47, literal).

Our expression of love must go out to the world around. Jesus requires that we feed the hungry, clothe the naked, visit the sick and the prisoner (Matt. 25:40). This is the "social action" which is preached so much from the pulpit, and practiced so little by the man or woman in the pew. Why? Because they have not yet been set free in the Holy Spirit to respond.

Francis of Assisi used to throw coins to the poor lepers,

[1]Cor. 16:20, KJV.
[2]1 Cor. 16:20, Phillips.

but after he allowed the Spirit of God to really work in his life (Francis was a "baptized in the Holy Spirit" Christian), he found that wasn't enough. He found he had to embrace and kiss these unfortunates. He had to use his hands to physically help them. Many are driven strictly by conscience to help the needy and oppressed in the world. The baptism in the Holy Spirit, however, opens people to relate to those in need, not just in protest marches, and subscriptions of funds, but in actually going to them with the love and comfort of God, ministering to them in the supernatural grace of the Spirit.

The Holy Spirit wants to move the whole person to go out in love to the world. If the physical body is held back, that work is seriously hampered.

24

Ladders Into Heaven

It is night on the desert. In the foreground a young man lies stretched on the sand, exhausted by hard travel under burning skies. His head is pillowed on a large flat stone over which he has thrown a sheepskin, a robe wrapped around him to keep out the chilly night air.

He dreams, and in his dream he sees a vast stairway or ladder stretching up and up, into the sky. At the top he sees a figure so bright that it's impossible to see the face, but he knows it is God Himself, and that the top of the ladder reaches right up to heaven. In his dream, the foot of the ladder is resting on the earth just a little distance away from him. As he stands gazing in wonder, he sees huge beings going up and coming down the ladder. They, too, are so dazzling he can hardly look at them, but he knows in his dream they are angels, messengers coming from heaven to earth and back again.

The dreamer of course is Jacob, and his experience is recorded in Genesis 28:11-13.

There's another interesting scene recorded at the end of

the first chapter of the Gospel according to John. Philip has just met Jesus, and has immediately gone to fetch his friend Nathanael. As Nathanael arrives, Jesus greets him: "Here comes a straightforward man who doesn't deceive others!"

Nathanael, much impressed, responds, "How do you know me?"

Jesus answers, "Before Philip called you, when you were under the fig tree, I saw you."

"Teacher," he exclaims, "you must be the Son of God! You're the king of Israel!"

Jesus surely smiled as He replied, "Are you so impressed because I saw you sitting in your own back yard? I tell you, you're going to see greater things than this. Why, you're going to see heaven open, and the angels of God ascending and descending upon the Son of man!"

Jesus was saying, "I'm the real fulfillment of Jacob's ladder. The glory of God will come down to earth through me, and the people on the earth are going to be able to come to heaven by me. I am the way from heaven to earth and from earth to heaven!"

When Jacob dreamed of the ladder and saw God standing at the top, God spoke to him and repeated the promise that He had previously given to Abraham, Jacob's grandfather (Gen. 12:2, 3), and to Isaac, Jacob's father (Gen. 26:4). To Jacob himself God said, "In you and your seed shall all families of the earth be blessed."

God had said to Abraham, "I will bless you . . . and you shall be a blessing . . . and in you shall all families of the earth be blessed." Now, what is the connection between "Jacob's ladder" and the blessing of "all the families of the earth"?

Paul picks up the theme in his letter to the Galatians

(3:6ff): "Abraham believed God and it was counted to him for righteousness. Know therefore that they which are of faith, the same are the children of Abraham. And the Scripture, foreseeing that God would justify the heathen through faith, preached before the gospel unto Abraham, saying, In you shall all nations be blessed . . . that the blessing of Abraham might come on the Gentiles through Jesus Christ; that we might receive the promise of the Spirit through faith. . . . Now to Abraham and his seed were the promises made. He said not, And to seeds, as of many; but as of one, And to your seed, which is Christ. . . . And if you are Christ's, then you are Abraham's seed, and heirs according to the promise."

Jesus was the fulfilment of the promise to Abraham. He was the chosen seed. While He was on earth He blessed all He could reach, then He ascended into heaven, so that He could empower millions of people, including you and me.

The diagram shown on the following page resembles a ladder, doesn't it?

And that's very appropriate, because everyone who has accepted Jesus is a little Jacob's ladder. Just as the glory of God came down to earth through Jesus when He was on the earth, so now the glory of God can come down to earth through each one of us who is in Jesus. We are now His body on earth. He depends on us to reach the world. He intends to pour out His love, blessing, healing, and joy through us.

So often at a meeting you'll hear someone say, "Jesus, please go and heal my mother," "Jesus, please go and save my 'unsaved loved ones.'" Or when praying for someone, you'll hear, "Jesus, please heal this person," "Jesus, please cast out this evil spirit." People feel somehow

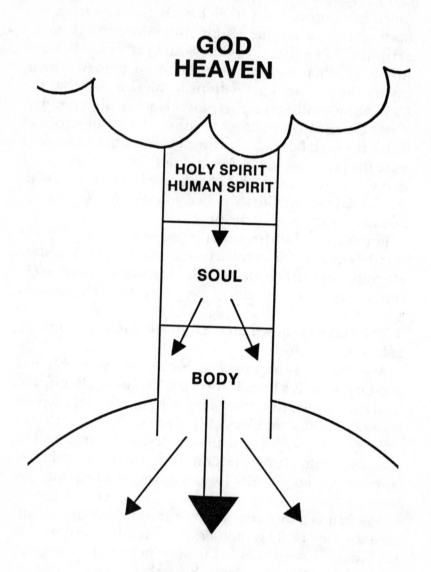

they've done their job as Christians when they've prayed for the people in India, or prayed for the president. Now, no way are we saying that we shouldn't pray or that prayer isn't effective. But let's remember that prayer is not asking God to go here and there and do things for us. Prayer is releasing the power of God *through* us to change circumstances. God works through our prayers. He isn't just waiting for us to tug His coat tails, and plead with Him before He'll do something. He cannot do all that He wants in a world that is still so much under the power of darkness, unless or until we allow His power to flow into the world from Him through us—through our spirits, souls, and bodies.

When your spirit opens up to God in faith, and then reaches out in prayer through your soul and body, God can work through you to change circumstances, to heal the sick, to bless the world. It is now possible for "all families" to be blessed because there are millions of God's people in the world through whom His Spirit can work—if we allow Him to. That's what this book has been about. We are the seed of Abraham by faith in Jesus Christ, and the promise to Abraham is given to us. We are first of all to be blessed, then to be blessings, and through us, all families of the earth are to be blessed.

When God promised Abraham He would bless the world through him, this is what He meant. Because Abraham was open in his faith, God could work through him by the power of the Holy Spirit, to begin to reach into the world that had become separated from Him and fallen into slavery to the devil.

We who are in Christ are the continuation of this process, only we have so much greater access to God's resources than Abraham did, for we can have the Holy

Spirit living in us. Our faith does not have to reach up to find God, for God has come to live in us. Heaven has come down into our own beings. As blocks in the soul are removed through understanding our triune nature, receiving soul healing, and other healing encounters with Jesus we will become more open and clearer channels.

If we allow the life of God in us to penetrate the barrier of the soul and to come right on through to "ground level," supernatural things can happen in the natural world. We are so used to operating "in the natural," that learning to let God come through and function in our everyday lives is not easy. We may have done our best to remove blocks in our souls and bodies, but we are learning a new skill, like learning to skate or ski. We keep falling down! But, as an old song put it, we "pick ourselves up, dust ourselves off, and start all over again!"

Most of us are still satisfied with occasional manifestations of the Spirit. We have the feeling: "Well, I got a miracle last month, I can't expect to live at that level all the time!" But if we want to see the supernatural love and power of God manifested every day, He must truly be Lord of our lives all the time. We've got to stay in fellowship with Him. When we are letting Him guide, things go so well that we wonder why we are ever satisfied to live any other way; but old habits are strong, and difficult to overcome. So we still too often say, "I'll take care of things during the day, Lord, and I'll see you tonight when I say my prayers—or at the prayer meeting on Wednesday, or in church on Sunday."

Yet it is as God's supernatural life comes through us that the world is going to see the "manifestation of the sons of God" (Rom. 8:19): that God is alive and real in His people, that He loves the world so much He sent His Son to rescue it, that the rescue operation is still going on, and that there is hope for the human race.

Francis Thompson, the man who wrote "The Hound of Heaven," caught the vision in his poem, "In No Strange Land":

> The angels keep their ancient places;—
> Turn but a stone, and start a wing!
> 'Tis ye, 'tis your estranged faces,
> That miss the many-splendored thing.
>
> But (when so sad thou canst not sadder)
> Cry;—and upon thy so sore loss
> Shall shine the traffic of Jacob's ladder
> Pitched betwixt Heaven and Charing Cross."[1]

Jesus was the ladder pitched between heaven and earth. The traffic of Jacob's ladder ascended and descended upon Him just as He had told Nathanael. Now through Jesus, we have become little "Jacob's ladders."

Wherever there is someone who is in Jesus, and is allowing God's Spirit to flow through him or her, there Jacob's ladder is set up between "Heaven and Charing Cross," between "Heaven and Main Street," or between Heaven and your kitchen, or Heaven and your office. Though your ladder is stationed on earth, the top of it reaches into "heavenly places in Christ Jesus" (Eph. 1:3). Wherever you are, the glory of God can flow down through you and out to the world to heal, to forgive, to bless. Through you—through us all—nations shall be blessed.

Let it be so.

---

[1]Charing Cross is the municipal center of London.

Bibliography

Dennis and Rita Bennett, *The Holy Spirit and You* (Plainfield, N.J.: Logos International, 1971).

Matthew Henry, *A Commentary on the Whole Bible* (New York: Revell).

Watchman Nee, *The Spiritual Man* (Great Britain: The Chaucer Press, Ltd., Bungay, Suffolk).

Thomas A. Harris, M.D., *I'm OK, You're OK* (New York, N.Y.: published by arrangement with Harper & Row Publishers, Inc., 1967).

Jamie Buckingham, *Risky Living* (Plainfield, N.J.: Logos International, 1976).

Dr. Robert Frost, *Set My Spirit Free* (Plainfield, N.J.: Logos International, 1973).

OTHER RECOMMENDED READING

Ruth Carter Stapleton, *The Gift of Inner Healing* (Waco, Texas: Word, Inc., 1976).

Ruth Carter Stapleton, *The Experience of Inner Healing* (Waco, Texas: Word, Inc., 1977).

Ed and Betty Tapscott, *Inner Healing Through Healing of Memories* (Houston, Texas, 1975).

Dennis and Matthew Linn, *Healing of Memories* (New York, N.Y.: Paulist Press, 1974).

Watchman Nee, *Release of the Spirit* (Great Britain: The Chaucer Press, Ltd., Bungay, Suffolk).

INDEX

We will be pleased to provide
locations of bookstores in your
area selling Logos titles.

Call: (201) 754-0745

Ask for bookstore information service